THE AMERICAN DREAM
A Constitutional Republic

Bill Koerner

authorHOUSE

AuthorHouse™
1663 Liberty Drive
Bloomington, IN 47403
www.authorhouse.com
Phone: 1-800-839-8640

First published by AuthorHouse   3/28/2011

ISBN: 978-1-4567-5341-2 (sc)
ISBN: 978-1-4567-5340-5 (e)

Library of Congress Control Number: 2011904499

Printed in the United States of America

Contents

Dedication and Introduction

Since the beginning of time Heavenly Father has raised up tyrants such as Nebuchadnezzar, Pharaoh and Herod to humble His people and to bring them back into remembrance of Him when they have strayed from obedience to His laws.

Our day is no different. We as a nation have turned against Him and His ways.

Hating the tyrants who rule over us is not the solution. They cannot prevail except as we, through rebellion against eternal principles, allow them power.

All that is necessary for evil to succeed is for good men to do nothing. Just as recent reports have told us that rapes have taken place in public streets while dozens of bystanders refused to give aid, so it is with our precious nation; we have allowed her to be raped and plundered while most of us have stood by without a word of protest.

This book is dedicated to all men and women who have fought in the battle for liberty whether on the battlefield in armed combat or in the battle for the minds of men against the perverters of truth who through the ages have enslaved nations by political intrigue, false education, and tyranny.

It is especially dedicated to my nephew Arthur Glen Hienen who was killed in Vietnam and my good friend Lt. Leo Abramoski who was killed in Korea. These two lives, along with tens of thousands of others, were lost in a valiant but fruitless effort to stem the tide of tyranny the world over.

While these noble Americans were laying down their lives in a war they were not allowed to win, the "American" news media were giving front-page coverage to insurrectionists in our country who were burning the American flag and praising the very enemies that were killing our boys.

Have you ever wondered why there were no heroes in Korea or Vietnam? There were! Just as many valiant deeds were done in those two wars as in any other, but the news media chose to ignore the nobility of these acts in preference to making a new type of hero for our youth to pattern their lives after – the drug-crazed "beatnik".

Have you ever heard of Wayne Coe of San Francisco, California, or Bill Anderson of Boise, Idaho, or Paul Anderson of Salt Lake City, Utah?

Probably you have not, though they were all highly decorated for valor and/or wounds received in combat.

Nevertheless, every American has heard of Jerry Rubins, Stokely Carmichael, Rap Brown, and Jane Fonda. All of these so-called Americans have praised the efforts of our enemies who were killing our boys on the battlefield.

These traitors were praised by every major newspaper and magazine in the country and were invited to speak at nearly every major university in an effort to lead the youth of this generation into an era of revolution against all authority, responsibility, and reverence for morality and freedom. The American public was led to believe that these police actions (Vietnam, Korea) were somehow needed to stem the tide of Communist conquest of the world yet in Korea our boys were being controlled, directed, and restricted by a Communist general. We fought that "police action" under the flag and direction of the United Nations. In Korea, the commanding officer was a Communist.

Since the inception of the United Nations in 1945, the commanding officer of the U.N. military forces has always been a Communist. Is it any wonder we were not allowed an ultimate victory?

We won the Vietnam War three times in the period I was there, 1967 – 1968, but the war was stopped and our troops disarmed for several days each time to allow the enemy time to rearm and reinforce their troops so it would look like a real war.

During the entire time of the Korean and Vietnam Wars, the Soviet Union and Red China were supplying all the equipment and much of the manpower needed to fight the war against our boys. Most disturbing however, is that during that time "American" industries associated with the Council of Foreign Relations were supplying all the materials needed by the Soviet Union and their allies for building the weapons, vehicles, and munitions used in killing our boys.

We all know that neither of these "police actions" was ever declared a war. We must ask ourselves how our youth could be committed to fight and die halfway around the world without our enemies being clearly identified or a war being declared by the Congress. The Constitution clearly states that <u>only Congress</u> can declare war and commit our citizens to fight such wars. Why was this legal requirement violated and who gained by such actions?

The safety and welfare of American service members is dependent upon the protection established in the Constitution by the Founding Fathers.

In times of declared war, no American can give aid or comfort to the enemy without being guilty of treason. If no war is declared, multibillion-dollar strategic sales can be made to our "unidentified" enemies without the stigma of treason. The Benjamin Spocks and Jane Fondas can visit the enemies' camps and cheer them on as was done in North Vietnam while the same enemies were killing our boys in South Vietnam. The news media would have us believe that they were not guilty of treason but that they were just good citizens doing some "public relations" work for détente.

How can any moral American stand by and allow such utter disregard for truth? Can we face those men and women who served in these <u>wars</u> knowing that we as a nation have betrayed them? Can we now continue to allow these same procedures to be used in other illegal military commitments around the world?

The Constitution is clear; it is not outmoded; it is restrictive against tyranny and treason. Treason and tyranny are, in the final analysis, what we are discussing.

It is one thing to require our youth to fight and die in pursuit of Victory over slavery and tyrants with the full support of their nation behind them. It is another matter when we require the same sacrifices of our service members with no hope of victory, with untold restrictions upon them, with their fellow citizens betraying them on every hand and with their own nation's leadership not allowing them the protection of the Constitutional safeguards.

These violations of moral decency on the part of our nation's leadership are merely a reflection of the moral decay of this once great nation and the fulfillment of the inspired words of William Penn who said, "Those people who are not governed by God will be governed by tyrants."

It was the political chicanery of both the Korean and Vietnam <u>Wars</u> that helped the author to realize the depraved condition of our beloved nation and also set him on the search for the reasons "why?"

This book contains many of the answers he found.

Purpose

The purpose of this work is to honor the Founding Fathers for their sacrifices and their worthiness to receive Divine guidance in the establishment of our free land and the creation of the founding documents that express the greatest principle of a just government ever written in the history of the world, The Constitution of the United States of America.

The founding fathers, who having lived under tyrannical government, understood that it is the nature of men (or women) that when they receive a little authority they begin to use unrighteous dominion over their fellowmen.

It was because of their experiences that they created the divinely inspired safeguards found in the Constitution.

Today, however, once more because of the lust for power and wealth, those called to authority have followed the age-old adage that power corrupts and absolute power corrupts absolutely, and they have chosen to violate every safeguard found in that great document.

For instance in ARTICLE 1, Section 9 of the Constitution we find that no State Legislature nor the Federal Congress can create a Bill of Attainder. (Laws of mass punishment)

As an example of such decrees, let us assume that we have a child in the eighth grade about to graduate that is taking the final exam for the class, and one of the classmates is caught cheating. If the teacher would stop the test and gather all the papers and would give every student a failing grade because of what one student did. That would be a Bill of Attainder. Anyone can see the injustice in such actions. Yet today because one man shot Mr. Brady, every person in America is deprived of the fundamental right to have and carry the weapons of their choice. That is an unconstitutional Bill of Attainder as are all other gun related restrictions found in our laws today.

This book has been compiled for the purpose of placing proper perspective on such activities and warning the citizens of our nation against the impending consequences of such violations of moral principles.

Preface

As a preface to some of the things we will cover, we must research the history of our beloved nation. In so doing we find in Jefferson's writings and in writings of others of our Founding Fathers that upon numerous occasions' heavenly intervention helped to establish this nation as a free land. These heavenly interventions came as a result of the prayers of these noble men.

How many of us realize that on one occasion George Washington was almost completely surrounded by the enemy; he had no hope of escape; he was cut off from all supplies and all assistance. All hope seemed to be gone. Then at that critical moment, a fog rolled in and blinded the enemy long enough for Washington and his troops to escape. On another occasion when he was encamped on a peninsula at the junction of two rivers, the British troops were sailing up the rivers on both sides and were about to execute a pincer movement behind Washington and his men. Then, just as the British were about to get into position, the wind ceased.

Their ships lay helpless in the water, and they began to drift down stream with the current because there was no wind with which to make the final move against Washington. He escaped again.

Most of us have never been taught that when the signers of the Declaration of Independence were contemplating the signing of that document, they began to hesitate, as well they might, realizing that the consequences of their actions would mean the death penalty if they were caught.

At the last moment, when they were about to give up, they heard a voice ring out from the balcony above them. The speaker gave one of the most inspiring speeches you will ever read.*[1] That speech was so moving that the Founding Fathers rushed forward eagerly and signed their names to the Declaration of Independence. When they had finished, they turned to thank the gentleman who had given the speech but he was gone. The doors were locked, the windows were barred, and there were guards posted all around the building; there had been no way for him to enter or leave unnoticed. Yet no one saw him enter or leave and no one knew who he was nor where he went.

Now these occurrences are recorded in a book entitled <u>The Secret Destiny of America</u> by Manley P. Hall.

According to another book entitled <u>Our Flag</u> by R.A. Campbell, we can probably deduce that this same gentleman appeared to Jefferson, Washington, and Franklin as they contemplated the design of our first flag. This was the first flag that the Americans fought under by direction of the Continental Congress. Not many know the design of that Flag. The Union Jack was in the place now occupied by the stars in our modern-day flag. Moreover, as we know, the Union Jack is the symbol of Great Britain. Is it not strange that the first flag we fought under had as a major part of its design the symbol of the country we were fighting?

1   Copy of <u>The Unknown Who Swayed the Signers of the Declaration of Independence.</u> See Annex "A"

That design was influenced by the gentleman known as "the professor" who appeared when they were discussing the design of the flag. They asked his opinion and he advised them to include the Union Jack in the design. He said that later the section then depicting the British symbol would be changed to "a field of blue that would be filled with stars as the heavens are at night," but he said, "for now put the Union Jack there and you will see the results in the war." Therefore, they designed it in that manner.

Three days later George Washington raised the new standard on the flagpole at Cambridge, Massachusetts. As it reached the top, the British army troops that were camped across the way viewed it through field glasses. When they saw its design, the British officers ordered a thirteen-gun salute in honor of that new flag.

The British soldiers began to realize that the Americans were not angry at England; they were not trying to sever all relationships; they still loved the mother country and wanted only to be independent of her. They still wanted to be considered as a friend.

The impact of the new flag began to weigh upon the minds of the British soldiers and eventually broke their will to fight to such an extent that Britain had to hire Hessian soldiers to help fight the war. It turned the tide of battle in favor of the Founding Fathers and helped ultimately to make victory possible.

It is essential for us to know that our Father in Heaven has a deep concern for our welfare and that He was the great motivating influence in the lives of our Founding Fathers. Today, for the most part, our nation and our leaders have forgotten the power of Him who made us free.

The gentleman who helped design the flag, referred to in Jefferson's journals as "the professor", assisted the Founding Fathers on other occasions also. Their writings show that he helped to establish some of the great principles of our original form of government. Thomas Paine and others who were there refer to this stranger. He came again and again to counsel them. The counsel that he gave them established the principles upon which this nation was founded, and thus the Constitution of the United States of America was created. The greatest document of government ever contrived by man, it was based upon the eternal principles of righteousness.

COLORS OF THE FLAG

When the Christ child was about to be born, his Mother, Mary prepared the manger in which He was to be laid. First, she took off the cape she wore, the symbol of her royal lineage. She was from the tribe of Judah of the royal line of King David and the color of the cape was royal blue. She took off this cape and laid it in the manger. Then she removed the white veil she wore indicating that she was a virgin pure and holy. She laid this white veil over the blue cape. Because she was also from the house of Boaz, she wore a shawl indicating the other side of her lineage. The family color of Boaz was red. She took the red shawl and laid it in the manger. Our nation's colors are a replica of the colors of the swaddling clothes upon which Christ was laid when He first entered into this world. It is clear that the foundation stones of this country were also based upon Christian principles!*2

The second flag under which the American troops fought displayed twelve stars arranged in a circle with one larger star in the center representing the house of Israel, the twelve tribes of Israel and their King, the Savior of the world and/or the twelve apostles and the Lord Jesus Christ.

(Later someone took it upon himself to redesign the flag and put all of the thirteen stars in the circle. This was not the design the "professor" originally communicated to the Founding Fathers. Therefore, when we go back and trace the real history of our land, we find that God had a hand in making America free.)

2   See "Jesus Christ in his Homeland Lectures by Mme. Lydia M. Von Finkelstein Mountford

We then can realize that He still has an interest in our liberty. He had an interest in our freedom then, and He has an interest in our freedom now. Do not ever think for a moment that liberty will not again be re-established and preserved by Him. It will be preserved, for God demands that His children be free if they but remember Him and keep His commandments. We are His children and we, if worthy, will remain free no matter what evil men of our day design to do, for Christ will prevail!

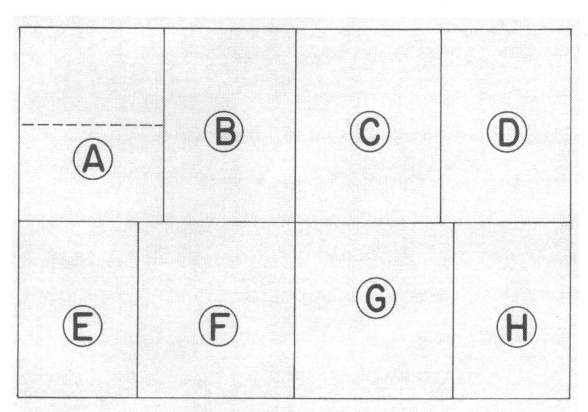

THE ABC'S OF GOVERNMENT

Chart 1

Chapter One

Constitutional Republic/Democracy

WHAT TYPE OF GOVERNMENT DID THE FOUNDING FATHERS GIVE US?

When Franklin came out of the Constitutional Convention, he was met by a little old lady who asked what kind of government they had given the country. He answered, "A Constitutional Republic if you can keep it."

What kind of government do we live under today? We are told that it is a Democracy. This should concern us because somewhere between the time of our Founding Fathers and today, our government has been changed! Have these changes given us more liberty or less? Have they enhanced our lives or restricted us more? Is a Democracy a better form of government than the inspired Constitutional Republic the Founding Fathers gave us?

As we consider these questions we must determine the true meaning of these two forms of government—a Constitutional Republic being that form of government that is based upon individual rights and delegated authority and a Democracy, based upon majority or mob rule. Let us explore these two critical concepts more in depth.

We must first determine what the original basis of our government was by studying Chart #1. This chart can easily be copied on a 3x5 card and carried in your pocket. If we can explain this one critical principle, we can explain to anyone where we as a nation have gone astray.

When Jamestown was first settled and when the pioneers came out west, they were like these individuals we have depicted on the chart. Let's pretend that all these men are farmers and ranchers, A,B,C, etc.

Rancher A moves to a new area and finds a parcel of land that he likes. He places a pile of rocks in each corner thus staking a claim and establishing it as his own property, or he purchases it from an earlier settler.

Later, when he has time, he builds a home with a fence around it. Then another family comes to the same general area and selects the piece next to him. They also construct a fence around their new land. Eventually there are several families in the same area, now constituting a community. Being an industrious people, they begin to develop the land and to produce.

There were also in those days, as in every generation, those that refused to produce for themselves and felt that they would rather take from those who did. There were Indian raiders and cattle rustlers, etc. This criminal element came into these areas and began to steal the commodities that those ranchers and farmers produced. Eventually, the landowners were spending so much time defending themselves against these intrusions that they could not pursue productive efforts.

They then decided to hire from among themselves one member to assume a full time defensive responsibility for them all. They decided to organize a government. They chose Rancher G to be that government. He became the first sheriff. Rancher G's duty was to ride around the entire community and protect all their rights and interests from intrusion.

Now he was required, because of his added duties, to give up his farming pursuits. The other ranchers therefore had to provide him with a good horse because he had to ride around all their property in one day. He needed a new saddle and a white hat so they could tell that he was the good guy. He also needed a badge, a gun, and all the other equipment that goes with being a sheriff. He could not afford to buy all this equipment and provide for his family unless he had some help as he had no other income after becoming sheriff. The people decided that they should tax themselves to support the sheriff and that they should all pay an equal amount because they would all be equally benefited by his efforts. His constant presence would constitute a threat to the criminal element and would discourage their unlawful activities.

Rancher A may have required his services more often than the other citizens because his property was located on the periphery of the community, but that fact had no bearing on the amount of tax paid because they were all being protected equally. Therefore, they were originally all taxed <u>equally.</u> That form of taxation is called a per capita tax. That is how taxes were originally levied according to the Constitution and that is the only legal and just tax on citizens, a <u>per capita </u>tax.

RIGHT TO KEEP AND BEAR ARMS

The next question that arises is, have the ranchers, because they have asked Rancher G to protect them, surrendered their right to protect themselves? Why should they surrender this right? It would be impossible for the sheriff to protect everybody at once. The only way for that to be possible would be for at least one deputy to be assigned to constantly guard every citizen in the community (or nation). The expense of such an undertaking would be prohibitive. Clearly, the right of the citizen to <u>keep and bear arms </u>is absolutely necessary for people to be secure against criminals in society and against the potential tyranny of government.

DELEGATED AUTHORITY

The next question is, how much authority does Rancher G have now that he is representing all these people? That is a very critical issue. How much authority can they give him? The answer is <u>only that authority which they themselves have.</u>

We can best illustrate this by the principle of power of attorney. My friend, Joye Wyatt, is a real estate agent. If I wanted her to sell <u>my home, </u>I could make out a power of attorney or a listing agreement with her to do so. But what if she sold your house instead? She would be in trouble and you would be in trouble too because you and your family would be out on the street.

The underlying principle, then, is that the agent (the government) can act only as the citizen can delegate authority for him to act. Otherwise, we would have chaos and all manner of illegal activities. Now let us look at that carefully to really see how it works because if we can understand this one paramount principle, we can understand the true basis of righteous government. We are talking about the individual's rights or how much authority the individual has, and more particularly, how much he can delegate to government; delegated authority is the basis of a government known as a <u>Constitutional Republic.</u>

PROPERTY RIGHTS

Let us take Rancher A for instance. Suppose he has a son who reaches majority and is about to be married. His father says, "I am going to give you an inheritance now so you can start your family. I am going to cut the property in half and give half to you….give you a bull and ten cattle….and start you out on your own farm."

He and his son are out driving fence posts to cut the property in half when Rancher B looks across the fence and says, "What are you folks doing?"

Rancher A answers, "well, we are subdividing the property."

Rancher B comes over, starts looking around, and says, "Why are you subdividing the property?"

Rancher A replies, "I am going to give my son half of it and he is going to build a home and start his own family."

The neighbor asks, "Where is he going to build his house?"

Rancher A responds, "Right up there by the river next to that big tree."

Rancher B says, "He can't build up there because he is going to mess up my environment and spoil my view of the mountain behind us, and I don't want him to build up there." Rancher B then begins kicking over the forms that Rancher A and his son have set for the foundation of the new home.

Now what do you think Rancher A would do with his neighbor? He would probably invite him off their property, and if he did not leave, he might even pick him up by the scruff of the neck and the seat of the pants and throw him over the fence. Why? Because Rancher B had no right on that property and in a true Republic that would be the end of it.

Today, however, in our supposed Democracy, Rancher B, would likely run over to Rancher C and Rancher D and get them stirred up because that new house would mess up their view also. So they would all run down to Rancher G and say, "We want a law passed that stops Rancher A from subdividing his property." As a result of their clamoring, Rancher G (the government) writes up a new "ordinance" stating that no one can subdivide his or her land into parcels smaller than say 50 acres. He rides over to Rancher A to tell him that he must stop what he is doing because of the new "law".

The question now arises; did Rancher B have the right or authority to forcibly stop Rancher A from cutting his property in half? If he had that right, where did he get it? What about Rancher C, D, E, etc? Did they have that authority? No. could Rancher B or any of the other ranchers then delegate such authority to Rancher G (government)? No. Then where would Rancher G get such authority? It could only be done by usurpation of power—going beyond the authority of the individual citizens.

In a Constitutional Republic, we believe in limited government….limited by what? By individual rights and authority. If I cannot do it to you without breaking the law then government cannot do it to you. <u>Government is limited by the authority the individual can delegate to it.</u> Does a group have any more authority than any individual does in that group? How could it? If I delegate my authority to you, then there is nothing more I can give you. I cannot create more authority out of nothing, nor can government! However, today in this Democracy, the government assumes or usurps more authority than the citizens have power to delegate to it.

The legality of the matter, however, does not rule out the possibility of solving the problem in a different way. Given a spirit of good will, the ranchers might be able to settle their own problems by voluntary negotiations among themselves without resorting to the unlawful force of government. Rancher A and his son might agree to move the house some distance this way or that in order to accommodate the desires of Rancher B. If neighbors can be friendly and not hostile, everybody gains.

However, if the parties cannot come to an agreement of their own free will, the ultimate right of decision as to use of the property remains with the owner except where eminent domain is at issue. The strict observance of the principles under girding liberty must take precedence over short-term gains for any one person or any one group. There is no good, no advantage, no apparent victory, no auspicious circumstance, no self-satisfaction that can in any degree, compensate for the miseries entailed in the loss of liberty.

LEGALIZED PLUNDER

Let us take another example: Rancher C's daughter becomes pregnant out of wedlock, an event common in our day, and she goes home upset and crying to her mother and father. They become very concerned that they will be humiliated in front of the whole community and they decide to go to Rancher D, the community doctor, and ask him to perform an abortion. The doctor agrees to do so for a fee of $500.00.

Rancher C does not have the $500.00 so, in his panic, he jumps on his horse and rides over to Ranchers A and B and robs them of $250.00 each. He then returns and pays Rancher D the $500.00. The doctor performs the abortion and everybody is happy, right? Of course not, Ranchers A and B have been deprived of their property unlawfully! They have been robbed, and under lawful government, Rancher C would be arrested and punished for armed robbery.

In our present "Democracy", we would have Rancher C and Rancher D joined by Rancher H, who has the same problem in his own family. In collusion with one another they would go around getting other people sufficiently excited about the issue to go to Rancher G (the government) with a supportive survey, and demand a tax increase on the most productive farmers for the purpose of easing the financial problems for Ranchers C and H and enriching Rancher D. They argue that Ranchers A and B enjoy better health than they, and therefore, in the interests of justice and kindness, their taxes should be increased to relieve the problems of Ranchers C and H.

These colluding ranchers would put political pressure on G to write an ordinance requiring a new tax levy increasing taxes for Ranchers A and B by $500.00 each. (You see, there must be a cost increase for the abortion because the government is involved now and must have money for salaries and administrative purposes). Rancher G "creates" this new tax levy under the "color of law," then he rides over to Ranchers A and B and extracts $500.00 from each one. He then pockets $500.00 for himself as pay for all the extra work he has had to do and gives the doctor the remaining $500.00. The doctor performs the abortion and everyone is happy. Right? Wrong, they have still been robbed, this time by "legalized plunder," and for double the amount originally needed to meet the problem.

Ranchers A and B would have been better off if Rancher C had robbed them directly. They would have escaped with only half the loss! Now, worse still, the new "law" has made this new tax increase permanent. In a Democracy, taxes are never decreased.

The way things are today, the extra tax money would probably be used to hire Ranchers C and H as government family counselors to advise children of other families in the community regarding the "virtues and advantages" of abortion without the knowledge and/or consent of their parents.

Now, remember, <u>neither Rancher C nor any other Rancher could rightfully force or deprive Rancher A and B of any amount of money to serve his own personal interests.</u> Therefore, he <u>could not rightfully delegate</u> to Rancher G the authority to do the job for him. When government assumes such powers, it is called legalized plunder!

The power of collecting and disbursing money at pleasure is the most dangerous power that can be entrusted to man. Out forebears understood this precept, at least up until the time of Davy Crockett.

When government functions properly, it protects the rights of the individual. By so doing it makes all society secure, for society is made up of individuals. However, if government attempts to satisfy the clamoring of special interest groups, whether minority or majority, at the expense of individual rights, all society eventually suffers the loss of all freedoms. In a Constitutional Republic, it is understood that an individual cannot delegate to government any more authority than he himself has. Now if we understood that clearly, we would realize the majority of all "laws" in America today are in violation of this basic moral principle.

The general acceptance of the abuse of this fundamental principle is the reason we are now called a Democracy. In reality, Democracy means mob rule. A Democracy assumes that if a group of people clamors for some special interest, the government can use that clamoring as their authority to write a "law" to deprive other individuals of their rights. Then the clamoring ceases for a moment until another group begins to clamor.

Today we live in a society, which teaches that such activities by government are acceptable. If "national surveys" indicate that the "majority" want a tax expenditure to finance the killing of the unborn, then that is the "authority" for the taxpayers to be burdened with such an abomination. Do we really believe that?

All government has to do is come up with more and more "surveys" in their favor to gain all power. Do we understand that this is what is happening to us? If we agree to such perverted reasoning, then we believe that as long as the "majority" says that immoral activities are moral, then it supposedly becomes moral. If the "majority" says that it is lawful to kill all children under two, or all African Americans, all Jews, all Native Americans, or all Christians, then wholesale murder or mass sterilization will become moral as long as the "majority" agrees to it.

This type of false philosophy is thought to be lawful in a Democracy, but anyone can see, after thinking it over, that it is not moral and therefore not lawful! Immorality is not changed into morality because the "majority" agrees to it! If we cloud the issue, which is what we are now doing, we will not move to free ourselves until all our necks are bowed beneath a cruel oppressor.

DUE PROCESS

If Rancher B feels free to demand that Rancher A give up his property rights to satisfy B's desire for a view of the mountain, then Rancher B must concede that he could be required to give up one or even all of his rights for that matter, to satisfy the selfish desires of someone else.

Once someone has purchased the property, he has free title and claim to it. It is his right to do as he will with it as long as it does not interfere with the rights of someone else and even that interference must be proven in a court of law.

Now if Rancher B wants to prove in a court of law that he has been deprived of his rights to life, liberty or property because of the actions of Rancher A, he must do so by due process. Let us say that Rancher A has his outhouse on the edge of B's property and he is accused of polluting the water. If that can be proven in a court of law, before a jury, with medical evidence that this is truly the case, then it can legally be decided accordingly. It could not however, be done by arbitrary and confiscatory legislation which is what we are discussing in the above examples.

PUBLIC SCHOOLS

Let us look at one more example in the A,B,C'S of Government.

Rancher A and his wife have been teaching their own children very successfully, so Rancher B offers to share the cost and also to provide a building to house the new school. They agree on educating their children together on a moral basis rooted in Christianity as well as the three R's---- Reading, wRiting, and aRithmetic.

One day Rancher C stops by and listens to the lessons Rancher A's wife is teaching her children and the children of Rancher B. C becomes extremely upset at the moral standards incorporated in the lessons and with the fact the student body begins each day with a prayer. He raises such a commotion that Rancher A and B rush to the school building to see what is happening.

Rancher C demands an end to the teaching of these moral precepts lest they rub off on <u>his</u> children. He has not wished for his children to be burdened with guilt for sin or for them to have worries over the consequences of any of their actions. "There is not a God," he says. "There is no right or wrong; all things are relative. Religion is the opiate of the masses," he raves and in his rage, he begins to destroy the materials and equipment of the school.

Finally Ranchers A and B subdue him physically and carry him out to his wagon advising him to teach his children what he will but to keep his nose out of their children's business.

Under the government of a Constitutional Republic this would be the end of the matter unless A and B would want to press charges against C for assault, trespassing, and destruction of property. However, not in a Democracy....

Today, Rancher C would run to his atheist neighbor H and together they would go to G (the government) with a new scheme for a public education system.

"While I was visiting one of the heathen nations," begins Rancher C explaining his plan to Rancher G, "I attended their institution of learning and acquired a Master's degree in atheism and amorality. We also found out that in many countries the three R's are really Rebellion, Rioting and Revolution."

"Why not pass a law making it mandatory that all parents <u>must</u> send their children to a newly-established government controlled school."

"Make me the Director of Public Education," continues Rancher C, "and make my standards the mandatory education standards."

"We could finance it by levying a new tax on all citizens. Maybe the tax could be on their income; that way the more productive they are, the more they pay. Even single persons who have no children in school could be taxed."

"If we can't get enough money by means of the income tax," explains C, "we could confiscate all their timber land and prime grazing land that belongs to the people and then lease it back to the ranchers for an additional source of revenue. We can also sell their timber back to them at whatever price we decide."

"We must be sure, however, to call all this confiscated land 'public land' so that we can dupe them into thinking that they somehow have something to say about it, not realizing that they have been robbed."

"We could steal their most beautiful areas, then call them National Parks and charge them camping fees and visiting fees when they visit these 'public' parks. We could require them to have licenses to hunt and fish on their own lands, to own and to drive vehicles and to trade or give services to one another; the possibilities are endless."

Note, we can all see that Rancher C's scheme is in full swing today. The government is the greatest property owner in the nation and also confiscates over half our income through some form of taxation or fees. In many of the western states over 80% of the territory within these states' boundaries has been unlawfully confiscated by the Federal Government under the guise of public lands. It is under the control of the Forest Service, Wilderness Areas, Bureau of Land Management, National Parks and Fish and Wildlife Refugees.

This arbitrary theft of property has been done in direct violation of the U.S. Constitution which clearly states that the Federal Government can control only <u>ten miles square for the seat of government</u> (Washington, D.C.) and other small areas clearly classified by usage for <u>erection of forts, magazines, arsenals, dockyards, and other buildings.</u> Nowhere is there authority for the ownership of over half of the land in the nation. It must be remembered that these lands were stolen through the abuse of the eminent domain clause and paid for by our own tax dollars. In other words, we are required to buy our own land from ourselves and then pay rental fees for its use and additional taxes to pay the salaries of those non-productive government workers who police us while we use these confiscated lands.

That my friend is legalized plunder of the first order.

"Another possibility for bilking the citizenry," continues C, "would be to create a property tax on everything they own. That way the citizens will never really own anything; they will just be leasing it from the government. If they cannot pay or refuse to pay the tax, we can imprison them or confiscate all they own for taxes. Eventually we would own everything and the citizens will work for us as our slaves instead of our being public servants."

Note, Jefferson said we should never allow government to establish a <u>property tax,</u> for if they have the power to tax property they also have the power to take that property from the people.

"With all these new taxes," continues C, "you, Rancher G, could double your salary because of the extra work you will have in policing law abiding citizens, instead of the criminals you were originally hired to police. You must make sure that all parents comply with our new educational

7

standards. You can also give me an income as Director of Public Education, so that I will no longer have to work at producing goods or services of value for a living. We can give Rancher H here a job as my assistant or as tax collector so he can also stop being productive."

"What if they insist on having their own home schools or private schools?" inquires Rancher G.

"Tell them they can still have private schools, but they must have their teachers trained and qualified by us, and they must teach the curriculum <u>we</u> establish. Explain also that they will still be required to pay the new taxes for education even though they gain no benefit from these taxes."

"I don't think Ranchers A and B will go along with that," says G. "They are pretty independent thinkers and they will see that their schools wouldn't really be private with all those controls."

"Then," says Rancher C, "we will just have to force them. Throw them into prison as they did in North Dakota and in Nebraska or shoot them in the back, if necessary, as they did in Utah a few years back when that John Singer fella stood up against their government schools."

Again we must ask ourselves, did Rancher C as a private citizen have the right to stop or change the educational program begun by Ranchers A and B for their own children? We can see that he did not. In order to accomplish this end, he would have been guilty of a series of crimes.

Are the criminal actions taken by government any less criminal than the same acts committed by an individual acting alone? How could they be? The harmful results are the same—only worse—because they have the force of law behind them.

If Rancher C had no right by himself to commit such acts, how could he assume that he had such authority as an agent of government? How could he assign such authority to another person to do what he himself had no authority to do? None of this can be done in righteousness!

Why then, does the government do these things to us? Because the government has usurped power through tyranny under the color of law or legalized plunder and we have allowed it.

Only a handful of courageous informed Americans have tried to expose this tyranny. They have paid dearly for their efforts.

Even a heathen or an atheist can see that although some think there is no God, jurisdiction must still remain with a Creator. If there were no God, the evidence is overwhelming that the parents are the creators of their own children. It is certain that the government has created nothing, certainly not our children.

If then we created our children, we have sole responsibility for their welfare, health, care and education, both intellectually and spiritually.

If officers of government desire to govern or be responsible for children, they can create them as we have done. There are plenty of government educators around to tell them how to do it.

Just because we have hired some few government officials to help us protect ourselves against criminals and to provide some common services, such as roads, postal service, fire protection, etc. we certainly haven't hired them to interfere in our family affairs or family government.

Family government is the foundation of all moral and secure societies!

Again, by this example, we can see how tyranny gets a foothold in every aspect of our lives if the citizens are not vigilant in controlling the force of government.

The government of men is not perfect; it requires safeguards. <u>The Constitution of the United States is the best system of safeguards ever established by men,</u> but we have not held our government to it. We have assumed that government actions are infallible and we have no responsibility for its actions except maybe to vote every few years and comply with government's edicts because "it's the law!"

It is this naïve and trusting nature of most Americans that has brought us to this dilemma, and for that, we cannot criticize or judge our fellow citizens. This trust will stand us in good stead when the judgments are finished and the Perfect Government we all yearn for is established. When He whose right it is to rule will rule in righteousness, America will be the first to accept Him and put all their trust and hopes in Him.

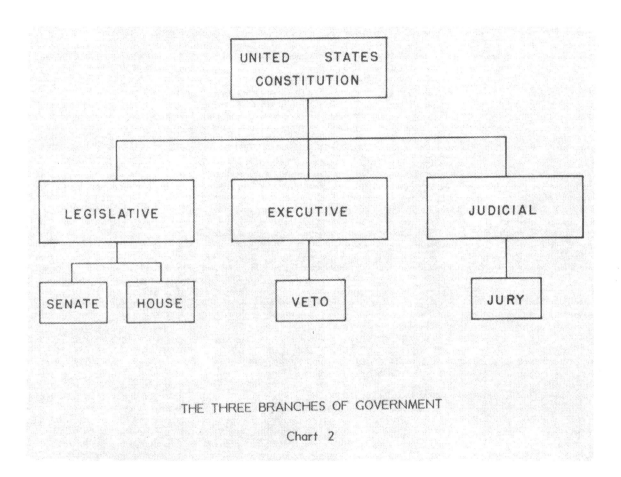

THE THREE BRANCHES OF GOVERNMENT

Chart 2

Chapter Two

The Three Branches of Government

We see on Chart #2 that the Founding Fathers also made sure that no individual and no one group of people received too much of the limited delegated authority. As an additional safeguard, they separated the power of government into three separate branches. Why did they do this? They knew that if the man who made the law had authority to judge those who broke "his" law, he would take a personal interest in it and would probably be more vindictive or more vengeful in his administration of punishment than a person who had no part in making the law. It was for this reason that they separated these powers into three separate branches. They knew that the amalgamation or centralization of powers would eventually lead to totalitarian control over the citizens.

The Legislative Branch was given the power to make all the laws, the Executive Branch was given power to administer the laws, and the Judicial Branch was to provide the forum where citizens could be tried by their peers for violations of the law.

LAW MAKING

ARTICLE I, Section 1, of the Constitution states that the Legislative Branch has power to make all laws....all laws. Who makes the laws today? The Executive Branch! It makes almost 90% of all laws. The majority of laws are made by Executive directives, statutes, regulations, office memorandums, and by Federal Register entries. The lawmaking (Legislative) Branch was meant to be an elected body directly responsible to those who elect its members. The Executive Branch has only two elected officers at the federal level....the President and the Vice President. All other officers are appointed.

Now if we have an appointed body of men making laws and they make bad laws, how do we get redress? We cannot because we have not the power to remove them from office. We are not able to vote them out at the next election because the Executive Branch, not elected by the people, appoints them. We can avoid troubles only by confining lawmaking to the Legislative Branch of government.

How many of us have seen the Legislature in operation? We should spend some time there to observe the lawmaking process. There are still a few laws made by that body. Some of us have been there often, and, if there were something we did not like in the proposed bill, we would put our names on a sheet of paper asking permission to speak before the house or senate committees. We would then be allowed to go in and give our testimonies and the reasons why we thought the law was wrong or right. Others could do the same. Both sides would have witnesses and testimonies from experts together with research programs to evaluate the bill to see if it would violate any of our rights or if it was really a beneficial law.

If then it passed through one of the houses, it was sent to the second house. The second house would review it from a different aspect. In case of a law being reviewed by the State Legislature, the interests of the counties would be considered. (That is until reapportionment came along—see Chart #3) If they amended it, then it would have to be sent back again to the other house for approval of the amendment. Back and forth and back and forth between these two bodies the deliberation of these bills would continue through many very careful checks, making it so that very few bad laws were passed.

USURPED AUTHORITY

Now let's suppose that we by-pass all these evaluations and checks, and someone sitting in the Executive Branch writes a new law the way he desires it (to control the people more efficiently) and there are no checks made on it, there are no deliberations or testimonies allowed and only the appointed official's opinion prevails. How safe are we with this procedure?

Today our government assumes that this method of lawmaking is just as protective as if the Legislative Branch had passed it. Do you think this is true? I do not. There is today, however, no objection to it; no one challenges such blatant violations of the separation of powers. These laws are written into existence without any safeguards. Appointed officers of the Executive Branch have brazenly usurped legislative authority in direct violation of the constitutional safeguards and the Supreme Court has been a party to it.

OSHA (UNBRIDLED POWER)

Here is an example: I have a son who works for a sawmill in Montana. While the saw is running, he is required by an OSHA "statute" to wear a hard hat. (Who has the authority to tell someone else what kind of hat to wear?) If an OSHA official happens to come by as he is taking his hat off to scratch his head, his boss can be penalized on the spot by a $100.00 fine!

Who wrote OSHA's directives? OSHA officials! What branch of government odes OSHA come under? The Executive Branch. Therefore, they have made their own "laws", and they now intrude upon industry and administer their own "laws". They are not even required to have a search warrant authorizing them to come onto a citizen's property.

A search warrant is a requirement of due process under the original constitutional concept, i.e. if a member of the Executive Branch suspects that there is a crime, he must go to the Judicial Branch and show probable cause. Then if he can convince an officer of the Judicial Branch that there may have been a crime committed, the judge will sign a warrant allowing the Executive officer to go onto the property to search for and to seize further evidence in the case.

OSHA does not go through the Judicial Branch of government. They trespass onto private property, and if they find that we have done something in violation of their alleged laws and/or ordinances, they fine us on the spot. What kind of power is that? What is a fine? It is a judgment. Who has the power to make judgment? The Judicial Branch of government has that power but only after a proper trial.

So here we have in OSHA a body of government that makes its own laws, administers its own laws, and designates and collects penalties for violations of its "own laws". Thus, all three branches of government are unlawfully consolidated into one body! What is that called? Totalitarianism! All offices of the Executive Branch now function this way, the IRS, HEW, HUD, OSHA. That is why patriots across the nation are challenging their unlawful acts. But the corrupt courts up to and including the Supreme Court have upheld these blatant violations of the Constitution and have sent thousands of our finest men and women to prison and even authorized the murders of some of them.

The Founding Fathers fought a long and costly war and suffered untold hardships to get free from such tyranny. That is why they separated these powers into three different branches. If all those powers are put back into one body, we are again threatened by unbridled power! "Bind them down with the chains of the Constitution," warned Jefferson. We have not heeded his warning.

The Founding Fathers also understood that when we elect a man to office, he does not become perfect over night. He will still make mistakes. They knew that if these officials made a mistake by passing an unjust law that could deprive citizens of their rights, they could vote them out of office. However, that was not enough of a safeguard. Even though the Executive Branch of government has veto power, the executive veto could still be overridden. (Veto power means that if the Executive Branch does not agree with the law passed by Congress, it can veto the law and send it back to Congress. It then requires two-thirds majority legislative vote by both houses to pass it into law.)

THE JURY, THE ULTIMATE CHECK

Let us suppose, then, that a terrible law is passed requiring that all children under the age of two be killed. All the police and soldiers start out murdering the children. Then one of the soldiers says, "Wait a minute, this is not right. I refuse to obey that 'law' because it is immoral." He stands by his convictions and he is picked up and dragged off to jail for breaking the "law".

The next day he appears before a judge and asks for a jury trial. The jury is seated and he says to the jury, "You can see that this law is immoral; it requires the taking of life which is in violation of the basic right of every person on earth." He convinces the jury that the "law" is immoral. The jury agrees and he is acquitted. What has the jury done? They have judged the law as to whether or not it is just or moral.

Recently I attended a school for judges, because I have been chosen to be our city's judge. It was a government school of course, and in that school, we were instructed in how to "properly" seat a jury. They stated that when a jury is to be called, we are to question them on these issues.

First, can the members of the jury accept the law as it is written? Can they put aside any personal prejudices, make no decision as to the morality or reasonableness of the law, and consider only whether the accused has broken the "law"?

What does that do? What the judge is saying to the jury is, if you can agree with the government and the laws created by the government, then you can sit on the jury. If you cannot put aside your personal feelings and your emotions as to the moral issues involved in the law, then you will be challenged out of the jury.

Let us suppose that a child is to be killed as a result of the "law", could you uphold such a "law"? If you as a jury member will not agree to sustain the government's position, you will not be seated on the jury. What does that do? It insures that only those who are willing to support the government, not considering the individual's rights nor the validity nor morality of the law, will be allowed to sit on the jury.

Talk about a stacked deck! That is jury tampering! John Jay, the first Supreme Court Justice, said, "The purpose of the jury was to keep control of government. The jury was to judge the morality of the law first." If the law is no good, why find the citizen who broke it guilty? He should be commended for his moral courage! The jury's primary interest then is first to make sure the law is just and moral. (For additional information, see the book, Trial by Jury by Lysander Spooner)

EDUCATION

If only we could educate all citizens in America to know that, they, as members of the jury, have the right to judge the law, as to whether or not it is a just or moral law and if it is properly made by the Legislative Branch! If every improperly made law, (that's about 95% of all the laws in the nation) and every law created by the wrong branch of government and never given proper review by those selected by us to do so, were to be judged by those informed citizens seated on a jury, how many of those laws would be found valid by that jury? Properly they should find valid only those few laws that are morally sound and passed by the correct body, the Congress.

Have we been robbed? We certainly have! Just as a thief might take one of our most prized possessions, we have been robbed of the right and privilege of exercising the final check in the administration of justice—the right to judge the law while seated on a jury!

The fundamental reason for our current predicament is that the citizens are taught in the government schools. We have allowed the government to take over the education of our children during the daytime, and the television to educate them during their leisure hours. The government is not going to tell anyone about the power the citizens have to control government, that power still remains in the hands of the people. Government officials want us to think that this is not true and that the government runs the country and we are the servants. The truth is just the opposite, but we have lost the concept of the people's being sovereign.

Red Beckman, who also lives in Montana, has traveled around our state teaching the citizens the truth about the power of the jury. The citizens in some of our counties are so well educated on the power of the jury that the federal government and the state agencies will not try any cases in those counties. They get a change of venue to another area because the government knows that there is too much understanding on the part of the informed citizens in these counties. The government knows that these informed citizens, sitting on the juries, will judge the morality of the law as well as the fact of whether or not the defendant broke the "law". They also know, that for the most part, the laws are immoral and would be ruled so by an informed jury.

There are then two powers of the jury. The first power or responsibility is to judge if the law is just or moral. The second is to determine if the accused is guilty of breaking the law. We must retain both of these powers by the jury in order to remain a free people! We must understand that nearly every court in our land is denying the jury this most important check against totalitarian government.

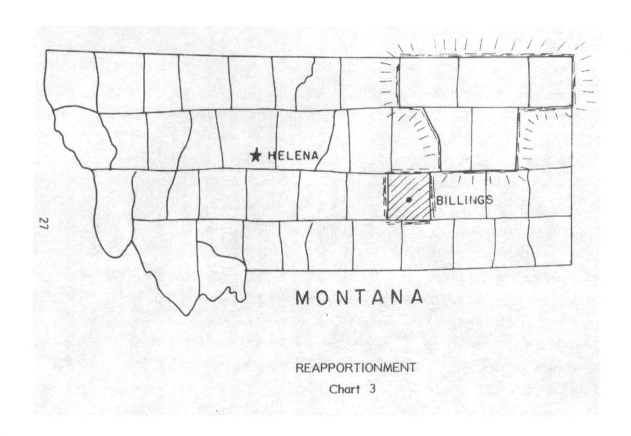

MONTANA

REAPPORTIONMENT
Chart 3

16

Chapter Three

Another Safeguard

First, then, we understood that originally government officials functioned only under delegated authority and that their delegated authority could not exceed the authority of the citizens they represented. Even that limited power was broken into three separate branches, so that no one body could exercise the whole of it. Then, as a further safeguard, we had an elected legislature that made a very careful scrutiny of all bills before they became law. We also had the check of veto power by the Executive Branch. Finally, the ultimate safeguard was the citizens' jury with the duty and authority to judge and strike down all unjust or immoral laws by the acquittal of the accused.

Originally, also as a safeguard, the Legislative Branch was made up of two houses. Why did the Founding Fathers establish two houses? They did so because the small states (small by population) were afraid that if the representation were chosen by population only, their interests would be overlooked or outvoted by the areas of large population. They would be outnumbered, and they realized that they would have little to say in making laws. As a result, the Founding Fathers decided to give each territory, state, or county equal vote in the Senate regardless of population. That way they all then had equal say in that body even though lesser-populated areas were outnumbered in the house where, as we stated, states and counties were apportioned according to population.

REAPPORTIONMENT
(UNCONSTITUTIONAL ACT OF THE SUPREME COURT)

It is easy to see what the subverters of liberty have done to our checks and balances. The last major change in our original form of government took place in 1967. The planned destruction of the final check against mob rule took place with the unconstitutional reapportionment decision by the Supreme Court in 1967. We had two separate houses. One was to represent the majority of the people who lived in the populated areas and the second was to protect the small, lesser-populated areas to the effect that all would have equal representation in the legislative bodies.

Prior to 1967 the fifty-six counties in Montana each had one senator to represent their interests so that no one could take away their rights by passing a law without their having equal voting power in the Senate. When the Supreme Court made the reapportionment ruling illegally and unconstitutionally, the five northeastern counties (outlined in Chart #3) were cattle-raising and farming counties. They are sparsely populated. Because of reapportionment, instead of having five senators to represent these five counties' interests, one for each county, they now have only one for all five counties.

Yellowstone County where Billings, Montana's largest city, is located, was given thirteen senators. What did that do to the balance of power?

That happened in every state. Today, more senators are chosen for the Legislature from counties containing large cities than from the lesser-populated counties in each state. We can easily see that the Supreme Court is not functioning as the defender of the Constitution. To the contrary, it has repeatedly ruled in direct opposition to its basic precepts. (For further information on the activities of the Supreme Court read <u>Nine Men Against America.</u>)

How wise the Founding Fathers were in retaining in the citizen's jury the power to judge the government and its laws.

FARMERS DISENFRANCHISED

Why did the Founding Fathers separate the two houses? They wanted to assure that the areas, which were small in population, would have the safeguard of equal representation in the Senate. Agricultural interests are important in this country, too. Have you wondered why the farmers are marching on Washington D.C.? Because no one cares! There is no one in the Legislature to protect them when the laws are made. Montana's predicament, with only one senator for all those five counties combined, compared with thirteen for one county with big cities, is similarly repeated all over the country, leaving the farmers, for all practical purposes, without any representation at all.

The house is made up the same way, of course. What we have now, then, is one house divided into two bodies. Members of each are elected by the same process and represent the same interests. Of course, they are going to agree with one another and they are not going to care about or defend the rights of the smaller-populated areas.

FOUNDATION DESTROYED

Can you see that all the basic foundation stones of a Constitutional Republic have been removed? All the things that the Founding Fathers fought and died for are gone! Power-hungry men who have usurped authority and set up, as a replacement, an alien system of government, have taken all the things that we have fought for since the beginning of our nation from us.

Chapter Four

Duties of a Just Government

WHAT CAN GOVERNMENT DO?

Having noted the many violations of government power in the past chapters, we must now explore the reasons for government and for JUST TAXATION.

According to our inspired Constitution, government is assigned certain specific duties and responsibilities. These duties are the lawful responsibilities of government. Citizens can <u>only</u> be justly taxed to provide these limited services. It must also be noted that <u>originally this tax had to be equally paid on a per-capita basis.</u> That is, each head of household paid his fair share for service and protection received and for being free.

CONSTITUTIONAL DUTIES

As we review these activities, we will see that as long as all citizens are blessed equally by the service it may come under the purview of government.

Government can according to the Constitution provide:

- Roads, Highways, and Postal service.
- Military forces to protect the nation, the calling forth of State Militia in time of declared war or insurrection at the National level, and police and fire protection etc. at the local level.
- The establishment of uniform weights and measures.
- Control of exports and imports.
- Protection for patents and copyrights.
- Courts (District and Appeal).
- Uniform rules of naturalization and laws of bankruptcies.
- Coinage of money and the regulation of the value (GOLD and SILVER ONLY).
- Punishment for counterfeiting.
- It can also define and punish piracies and felonies committed on the high seas and offences against the law of nations.
- Declare war, grant letters of marque and reprisal, and make rules concerning captures on land and water.
- Raise and support armies.

- Provide and maintain a Navy.
- Make rules for the government and regulation of the land and naval forces (not the civilian citizen).
- Provide for calling forth the militias (State) to execute the laws of the Union, suppress insurrection and repel invasions.
- Provide for the organizing, arming and disciplining of militia and for GOVERNING <u>SUCH PART</u> OF THEM AS MAY BE EMPLOYED IN THE SERVICE OF THE UNITED STATES.
- Exercise exclusive legislation in all cases whatsoever, over such districts (NOT EXCEEDING TEN MILES SQUARE) (Washington D.C.) as seat of government and like authority over places which shall be for the erection of forts, magazines, arsenals, dock yards and other needful buildings. (No parks, forests, wilderness areas, game refuges, or grazing lands etc. are anywhere authorized!) All other responsibilities are specifically left to the people and/or to the States.

ALL STATES MUST PROVIDE A CONSTITUTIONAL REPUBLIC FORM OF GOVERNMENT

In addition to the above listed duties, the Federal government is assigned the responsibility for MAKING SURE THAT THE STATES ALSO PROVIDE A REPUBLIC FORM OF GOVERNMENT FOR THEIR CITIZENS. That form of government is based on the common law, or God's law.

We can see by the simple outline clearly stated in the inspired Constitution that nowhere is government authorized or assigned the responsibility of taking care of the housing needs of the people, regulating farm or industrial production, feeding the poor, educating the children or in any way interfering in the family or personal lives of the citizens. All such responsibilities and needs were to be left to the families and to the charitable acts of the people themselves or to their cooperative efforts by each sacrificing for others of their own free will and choice.

When government is limited to these few areas of service or protection, each citizen would be happy to pay his fair share through a just tax. However, even if a citizen chose not to pay his fair share, he merely would not receive the service, i.e., fire protection, police protection, etc. leaving him to his own devices without materially effecting the remainder of the society.

NO DEBTORS' PRISON AUTHORIZED

There never was meant to be a debtors' prison (as there is today) in our nation. Thousands of American patriots have or are now serving time in debtors' prison for resisting the unjust, immoral tax system and hundreds of other corrupt laws imposed upon us. These patriots sustain Jefferson's position of "Resistance to tyrants is obedience to God."

We as citizens could not have another citizen jailed for a debt owed us, only government has usurped such power over us to support their unlawful tax system.

RESISTANCE TO TYRANNY

Unjust imposition of government power is bullying in its lowest form. Today thousands of Americans are attempting to resist tyranny by standing up against the usurped powers of unlawful taxation and education, and against government edicts that rob us of our property rights, freedom of religion and jurisdiction over our own flesh and blood (our families).

These patriots are suffering untold hardships and abuse at the hands of government agents from the IRS, HUD, HEW, E.P.A., B.A.T.F. and other unconstitutional organizations of oppression.

Thousands are now in prisons or have lost all they have in the battle for freedom while most of our citizens stand by idle not attempting to lift a hand or to utter a word in their defense.

It is impossible for me to comprehend such lack of dedication or concern for our fellow citizens. I can only liken it to those who would stand by and do nothing while a woman is raped or robbed and beaten on the streets of our cities. I shudder to think of the eternal consequence of such cowardice.

JUST TAXATION

<u>Just taxation for government functions must be limited to those areas where all persons taxed are serviced or protected equally by the government activity paid for by the tax,</u> i.e. police and fire protection, road and postal service. Such services benefit all the citizens that are paying the tax.

ANY TAXES THAT ARE USED TO BENEFIT SOMEONE OTHER THAN THOSE TAXED ARE UNJUST OR LEGALIZED PLUNDER. Any such needs should be left to the free will or charitable acts of the citizens without force or coercion on the part of government.

BONDING ISSUES ARE ILLEGAL

Let us take school bonding issues as an example. Today local governments assume the authority to tax all property holders within a given school district to satisfy a bond to build or expand school facilities.

In addition to the fact that property taxes are unconstitutional, we have several other illegal aspects to such propositions. First only property holders will be saddled with the payment <u>while non-property owners can still vote on the issue to impose the tax.</u> In other words, we have representation without taxation, which is just as unjust as taxation without representation. That is why property taxes are unjust!

PRODUCTIVE CITIZENS SADDLED WITH RESPONSIBILITIES OF OTHERS' CHILDREN

Secondly, we have property holders saddled with a tax increase for which many receive no service or protection. Any property owner who has no children in public schools or no children at all is required to support other families who choose to put their children in government schools.

Properly those who choose to place their children under government schools should be required to pay the FULL cost, just as those who choose the private school program are required to do for their children. These principles are so simple, as is all truth; even a child could understand them. It is difficult to understand how we have allowed these simple truths to be so perverted in our day.

DEBT

Another aspect is that of debt. To construct a $100,000.00 dollar building today on a 20 year bond at 10% interest would cost the tax-payer in reality $300,000.00 or more, or three times the actual <u>reported cost</u> in the bonding vote. If we ran our personal businesses at such a deficit, we would be forever in debt.

Government spending should be limited to the funds on hand except in cases of emergency for national security. If a local government needs new facilities that would serve all the people in that tax district equally (school facilities do not fall in that category), it should plan enough ahead to hold a portion of the present tax monies each year in a savings account ear-marked for the building project. These funds then could draw interest in the saving period and thereby not only save the taxpayer the double or triple cost caused by interest in deficit spending, but additionally cut the cost to the taxpayer by the amount of interest accrued on the money in the savings account. We have no right to indenture the next generation for our folly.

SOLUTION TO SPECIAL INTEREST PROBLEMS

If some of the citizens want a school building, they have several options. The school officials can charge a fee to ALL THE PARENTS OF CHILDREN INVOLVED IN THE SCHOOL ON AN EQUAL SHARE BASIS THRU A DIRECT LEVY. Others who desire to help may voluntarily donate money, equipment, material, and/or labor <u>of their own</u> for the construction of the new building. This is the American Dream, personal responsibility and voluntary charitable acts on the part of concerned citizens to bring about such special interest projects.

It should be noted that in spite of the material covered on resistance to tyranny and just taxation, this chapter is very short indicating that the duties of government, which are constitutional, are indeed very few. Good government then allows for the widest latitude of liberty and freedom of action for the citizens. "That government which governs least governs best." This is a true Republic or "The American Dream".

Chapter Five

Weights and Measures

There is further evidence that the Founding Fathers were divinely inspired because they chose to adopt the inch, foot, and yard measurement system for our nation. Today there is a multi-billion dollar push to force upon us the mathematically unsound metric system.

THE PYRAMID INCH

Let us review the original measurement system: The original inch measurement is found in the great Pyramid of Giza, one of the Seven Wonders of the World. It therefore has historically existed for more than five thousand years and survived all attempts to pervert it.

This inch measurement is found on the granite leaf in the entrance to the King's Chamber of the Great Pyramid as a portion of stone that juts out from the surface and is called THE BOSS. It is exactly one inch thick and is shaped like a horseshoe.

THE BOSS

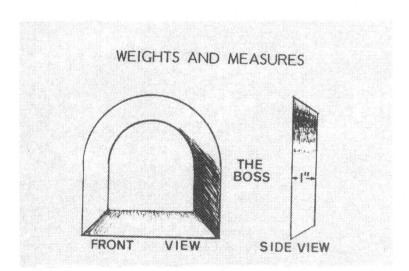

The volume of the Boss is one Winchester pint. One Winchester pint of water, at mean temperature, at sea level weighs one pound. There-by comes the old saying, "A pint's a pound the world around."

The Great Pyramid is a record of the Bible and its prophecies committed to stone by the Servants of God. All other pyramids are attempts to copy the original.

THE DIVINE MEASUREMENTS

In the Boss, then, was recorded not only the distance measurement of the inch but also the volume, the temperature, and the weights used by the ancient believers in God. The inch is established also in the foot; there are twelve inches to remind us that there were twelve tribes of Israel and twelve apostles of the Lord Jesus Christ.

There were three feet in the yard to call to our remembrance the three members of the Godhead (Father, Son, and the Holy Ghost).

THE ORIGIN: INCH vs. METER

One inch is based upon the celestial measurement of our earth's diameter through its north – south axis. That is if we were to drop a plummet through the earth from the North Pole through the South Pole, which is a known calculable distance, one inch will be found to be 1/50,000,000th of that distance. The meter, on the other hand, is purported to be 1/10,000,000 of the distance from the North Pole to the Equator around the earth's periphery. The first obvious deficiency then is the fineness or accuracy of a measurement that is 1/10,000,000 versus the critical accuracy of a breakdown of 1/50,000,000.

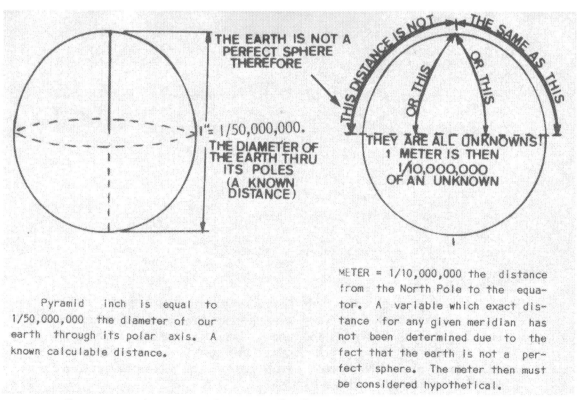

Pyramid inch is equal to 1/50,000,000 the diameter of our earth through its polar axis. A known calculable distance.

METER = 1/10,000,000 the distance from the North Pole to the equator. A variable which exact distance for any given meridian has not been determined due to the fact that the earth is not a perfect sphere. The meter then must be considered hypothetical.

Secondly, even an elementary education will tell us that the earth is not a perfect sphere but rather is pear-shaped. Any measurements made around the peripheral or outside curvature of the earth would vary according to the direction taken or the meridian followed from the North Pole to the Equator.

For those who have been led to believe that the decimal increments of the metric system are the justification for the multi-billion dollar sales expenditures to propagandize this program, it should be noted that the Lord understood the decimal system from the beginning of time. Decimals existed long before the metric system was ever thought of. Any engineer will verify that the increments of tenths, hundredths, and thousandths of a foot have been used since the earliest records of man. It is found in every engineering office on the engineer scale.

Again, let us remember that the meter is in reality an unknown commodity so we can conclude that one-tenth, one-hundredth or even one-millionth of an unknown is still an unknown!

The metric system and those who have been brain-washed into having faith in it are just that much more evidence of the false precepts taught in our public schools and one more reason why we should shun government schools as we would the very gates of hell.

Why would any person desire to change a proven system of measurement to an unsound system, without foundation in reality, unless they were determined to destroy the weights and measurements, revealed by God to His people, or were attempting to destroy their identity?

GOD'S PECULIAR PEOPLE

Throughout the history of the world, then, these measurements established all who used them as a peculiar people who believed in the true God. All other systems are counterfeit. The pyramid inch and its associated measurements were revealed to the world by God through His prophets and were meant to identify those who believed in Him. They were also meant to remind us daily of who we are and who our God is.

Our God is the same God who stood by Daniel in the lions' den and by the three Hebrews in the fiery furnace. He strengthened David in his battle with Goliath and Joshua in the war of liberation of the Promised Land.

He is the God of miracles who delivered the children of Israel from bondage in Egypt in their day. He also delivered our country's Founding Fathers from the hands of their oppressors. He will yet deliver us from those who would enslave us in our day for He is the same yesterday, today, and forever.

He is waiting for a people who will again put their trust and faith in Him and His delivering power. A people who fear not man nor what governments can do. A people who hold inviolate the rights of men and the virtue of truth and justice.

When He finds such a people, He will come and set up His perfect Kingdom among them, a Kingdom of righteousness that will never end. This truth is more certain than the rising of tomorrow's sun.

Chapter Six

Other Principles

COMMON LAW / LAW OF EQUITY

The common law or God's law holds every individual's rights inviolate. No one can cross family lines except in defense of life, liberty, or property, in consequence of some willful act in direct violation of these individual rights. Such rights are clearly identified in the Declaration of Independence as inalienable rights bequeathed us by our Creator.

The law of equity is based upon the premise of, that which is best for the most holds precedence over individual rights. Let us review some examples:

OUR P.O.W.'S

When our boys who were in prison camps in Vietnam or Korea were interviewed upon their release, many related the following or similar stories.

They were put in small buildings about the size of an average living room. There were usually 30 to 40 people crowded into each of these ill-constructed buildings. There was no heat or insulation and no way of keeping themselves warm. The winters in Korea are extremely cold. The prisoners were clothed in denim type clothing with no heavy coats or blankets to protect them from the weather. Their bunks were stacked closely around the walls, with little or no free space. The food was poor and of little quantity.

Living under these conditions, eventually one of the prisoners would contract dysentery. If this condition is not treated, within a month or two, the victim will die of dehydration. In a close situation such as this, the sickness would spread rapidly to other members in the building as a result of the unsanitary conditions that existed.

The Communists would tell the prisoners, "If you don't want to contract dysentery, from those individuals who have the disease, you as a group must decide to throw the sick outside in the freezing weather." If the group did not single out the individuals who were ill and put them out, the healthy individuals would run the certain risk of sickness and death themselves.

THE DECISION

When more and more of their numbers became ill, and there was no apparent chance of making them well, the group would elect to put the sick members out in the freezing weather to die. As a result, weeks or months later the reality of the terrible decision they had made came back to haunt them. The realization that they had been a party to the murder of their brothers and comrades was more than their conscience could handle. Many eventually broke down mentally and admitted to anything the Communists ask of them. This is why many or our boys would admit to immoral acts and other things that they really did not do. This then is the method the Communists used to break down the moral standards of our service members, and to force them to accept the law of equity, first in their minds and finally in their actions.

EQUITY ONLY TAUGHT IN THE PUBLIC SCHOOLS

Similar tactics are being used for the destruction of the moral standards of our youth in the public schools. Several years ago, one of my sons came home one evening and asked me to help him solve a problem, which was given to him in school. The problem was that there was going to be an immediate atomic attack and you are living in a large city. Your family has a bomb shelter in the back yard and so you and one of your children rush for the safety of the shelter along with some of the neighbors who have knowledge of the bomb shelter. The door is shut, a tremendous explosion occurs, and at the end of the third day static on the radio finally ceases and a faint voice announces that the city has been hit with a massive atomic attack. The city has been leveled. You are instructed to stay in your shelter and not come out for 30 days, to allow the radiation to dissipate. You look around and discover that there are eleven people in the shelter with you and after an inventory of the food, you discover that there is only enough food for six people for the 30 day duration.

The problem asks that the child write an essay in which he is to decide which five people should be thrown outside into the radiation to die, and the reasons why. Each of the individuals is described along with special information, such as their age, education, sex, beliefs, etc. One person is described as being a strong young black man who is the only one who has the strength to move the heavy iron door on the shelter. Another would be an elderly person in their 70's who was in poor health, another a woman who is pregnant, while another might be an individual who is handicapped.

WHO WILL LIVE AND WHO WILL DIE

The frightening thing is that every public school in America asks our young people to visualize this type of situation and to make these life and death decisions. The individual choices or details are not clear-cut for the children to make, but the verdict is directed leaving the final decision up to the children. <u>Who will live, and who will die?</u>

THE SINKING SHIP

Another decision making story told to our children is about a large ship which is sinking. There are many people on the ship and after the ship has been rammed, only three of the lifeboats are in operating condition. The story goes that you are in the lifeboat and as the ship is sinking 30 people surround the lifeboat and want to be rescued from drowning but the capacity of the lifeboat is only 16 persons. Again the people in the water are described and our children are once more required to make a life and death decision regarding the people involved.

These stories are a part of the educational standards of the public schools in America today. What are these schools trying to teach our children? They are teaching the children to make decisions as to whose life is important and whose can be taken. Considering the words of the Scriptures, "As a man thinketh, so is he," our children are being trained to think as murderers! This is not a decision for man to make except in capital crimes. This decision is a decision reserved to God only!

The teachers cannot offer the children white and black decisions. The answers are always a choice between two black areas such as you must kill five or you must kill twenty.

THE MORAL SOLUTIONS

There are other logical and moral solutions to the examples above protecting the rights of each individual. In the first case, the solution to feeding all those in the bomb shelter is that the people fast every other day thereby providing enough food for all involved. In the second case involving the lifeboat, would it not be logical, that half of the people could be in the boat and one half be in the water hanging on to ropes or the edge of the boat and taking turns at regular intervals?

We also have the option of those involved voluntarily giving their life in sacrifice for the welfare of others. We have actual examples of such situations, one not too long ago when a commercial aircraft failed to clear a bridge on take-off at Washington D.C. It was in the dead of winter the plane sank into the frozen Potomac River.

A REAL LIFE EXAMPLE

All should remember the heroic sacrifice of an unidentified citizen who, each time the rescue helicopter returned to pick up a survivor, gave his place to another less strong than he, again and again this nobleman gave up his chance to live, to another.

Finally, all known survivors had been picked up and the helicopter returned to rescue him, he was gone. How more perfectly can we describe the spirit of Christianity?

JACOB HAMBLIN

One other example is that of pioneer, settler Jacob Hamblin who found himself in a life and death situation with the Navajo Indians.

One of his company had been mortally wounded by the hostiles and they said they wanted two more white people to kill, to even the score for some previous loss the Indians had suffered in an assault on a pioneer wagon train.

Outnumbered, Hamblin was faced with the decision of surrendering two of his companions into the hands of the Indians or suffer the death of the entire group.

He says in his account of the happening of that confrontation that he retired and prayed to Heavenly Father for strength. He returned to the main group and said, "We will ride on together regardless of what they do, for I would rather die as a man, than live as a dog by surrendering the lives of two of our number to save our own skins."

They rode on to safety harassed but untouched by the Indians.

Later at another such confrontation the same Indian-leader who was present at the first meeting told Hamblin that his courage had won the respect of the Navajo and they form that time on considered him their friend and brother.

In all these stories, moral principles would make the difference.

MORALITY CANNOT BE TAUGHT, IMMORALITY CAN. "IT'S THE LAW!"

These precepts of personal sacrifice and religious faith cannot be discussed in a public school because the teacher would then be teaching a religious or moral concept. As a result, they are required to teach the false religion of materialistic humanism or that it is proper to kill five people in the bomb shelter or murder fourteen individuals in the lifeboat episode. In both cases what is best for the most? The ones remaining in the shelter or on the boat out-number those who lose their lives and therefore according to the law of equity or majority rule these actions are justified. However, the real question is, does that make these actions moral or acceptable before God? Of course not. The moral position of Christianity is this. Christ said, "Greater love hath no man than he (voluntarily) lay down his life for a friend." The teaching of Lucifer is, "If you can survive or if you can gain by it, kill the other guy." This is the theme of materialistic humanism as taught in the public schools. It is taught in our schools in place of morality because it supposedly is best for the most and that is "democracy" or equity law.

LOSS OF JURISDICTION

A parent automatically submits to and authorizes his children to be taught these types of un-godly principles when he or she voluntarily enroll their children in the public schools of America. Why is this so? Because when the "government" through mass taxation is paying the bill for the public schools and the "government", the majority or some powerful special interest minority, deems these principles valuable. They become part of the government educational standards for the youth of America.

There is no place for government involvement in the education of our children in a moral society or a Constitutional Republic.

If you choose to send your children to public schools, you are relinquishing your right to control the subjects taught to them because you have given up your jurisdiction over your children to the majority. The majority of the people are paying the bill for the education and therefore in "a democracy" the majority has the right to determine what will be taught in the schools under the law of equity. Your voice is only counted as one of millions and carries only that weight. Your individual inalienable rights no longer exist under such a perverted concept.

The entire question of government then boils down to jurisdiction. Who has jurisdiction over your person and of your family?

FREEDOM IS RESPONSIBILITY

GOD ON THE ONE HAND MAKES US FREE AND WITH THAT FREEDOM MAKES us responsible to Him for our own and our family's welfare, housing, education, food, clothing etc. On the other hand the anti-Christ and men who don't believe in God would have us believe we are not capable of this responsibility and they, "the intelligent ones", will have to make all these decisions and assume all these responsibilities for us. They then steal money from the people to accomplish this enslavement process through unlawful taxation. From this comes the statement, "all men are equal except that some ('the intelligent ones') are a little more equal than others". All they ask is for us to surrender our liberties and our jurisdiction to them and be subservient to them.

THE BAIT AND THE HOOK

There always appears to be many advantages to taking these government controlled funds and "free" services offered. On the surface, it appears that nothing is lost and all is to be gained. This "free money" (taken from someone else through theft) gives the illusion of a cornucopia of endless funds with which we can do all the things we ever dreamed. The truth of the matter is that the minute the money changes hands the jurisdiction over our lives is surrendered to "majority rule". ALL WE HAVE TO DO IS RELINQUISH OR SURRENDER OUR JURISDICTION OVER OUR OWN FLESH AND BLOOD AND OURSELVES TO THE MAJORITY!

STILL SLAVES

We fought a costly civil war to abolish slavery, now more than half our population has voluntarily put themselves back into slavery for a government handout. To many, money means more than freedom!

In the above stories the premise is that if five must be killed in order that six may survive, then it is a worthy cause and according to the anti-Christ or dialectic materialism that is fair. The law of equity is a continuation of this philosophy into government. The law of God, on the other hand, allows us to give our lives for the cause of liberty or to voluntarily lay down our lives for a friend etc. However, these actions are our own choice under free agency. We deal with our own lives and not the lives of others. There is a vast difference between doing an act voluntarily and forced to do so by another or by government "laws".

OUR SPACESHIP WORLD

A third story taught to our children is one where the earth, described as a spaceship has only enough room on the spaceship to grow a certain amount of food. When the population on the spaceship reaches the maximum number that can be fed by the food produced, then again under the theory of what is best for the most, we will need to sterilize the parents to restrict the birth of more children or terminate the elderly for "they have outlived their usefulness". The commanding force of the spaceship would take this action.

The parallel in real life is that because of "overpopulation" the government has authority to demand that the size of the family unit be restricted by involuntary sterilization of the people under supervision of government officials. This action is again "justified" under the premise of what is best for the most which of course is equity law or mob rule. If the woman becomes pregnant without the consent of the government, the only answer is abortion as is done in China today. According to this barbaric theory, it matters not if the baby is to be born in days, weeks, or months. This murdering of the old and the unborn will be justified under the guise of equity law. Those responsible for the murders will be upheld by the government as not guilty according to the plan of Lucifer. These are the types of life and death decisions that our children are forced to make each day in our public schools. It is designed to mentally prepare our youth to make decisions of mass murder and be justified in their own minds for their actions without regard for the moral principles involved or the eternal consequences of their actions.

THE OVER-POPULATION HOAX EXPOSED

The hoax of over-population can be easily dispelled if one considers the true mathematics of it.

I live in Ravalli County, Montana. The county is approximately 90 miles long, north to south, and about 15 miles wide. If all the people on earth today were put into the boundaries of this county, they could all fit without touching each other.

If we were to construct a city, to house all the people on earth, with the population density of New York City, it would be the size of our sister state of Washington. The over-population scare is also part of the plan to enslave the entire world under the dictatorship of the anti-Christ.

MAJORITY VOTE SOMETIMES LEGAL

We must understand that in a Constitutional Republic there are a few legal areas where majority vote would hold sway.

Those areas are clearly outlined in our inspired Constitution. It is limited to election of our representatives and to the legislative process in areas of protection and service to all citizens equally.

That is, the Congress or State Legislatures can by majority vote of both houses, enact such laws that protect or serve all the citizens within their jurisdiction equally, but ONLY IN THOSE AREAS SPECIFICALLY ENUMERATED IN THE CONSTITUTION.

We can easily see where such areas of LIMITED FEDERAL AND STATE government under a CONSTITUTIONAL REPUBLIC have been expanded to a totally alien system of "democratic socialism."

TRANSITION TO GOD'S KINGDOM

It would have required only a few minor changes to the original limited system of government of a Constitutional Republic to establish the Theocratic Republic of God's Kingdom on His return.

Under such a government, the King of Kings would uphold the perfect unchanging Constitution with His perfect wisdom and justice by His veto power over the Representatives of the people.

Now however, instead of a peaceful transition it will require the total cleansing of the nation of all its unrighteous laws and actions before Christ's Millennial Reign can be ushered in.

It is imperative that those who understand this divine plan of government as established by the Founders of our Nation, preserve and maintain it undefiled in their own areas and in their own families and lives.

God must have a people who will place MORALITY IN GOVERNMENT AS WELL AS MORALITY IN THEIR PERSONAL LIVES ABOVE ALL THINGS before He can come and establish His Kingdom among them.

If we were to consider the possibilities of taking "government funds" or partaking of some program or service, <u>outside the constitutional jurisdiction of government,</u> such as public education, grants, welfare, etc., we must first consider where money or assistance comes from.

There are only two sources of assistance to provide for our sustenance in life. One source comes from our Father in Heaven through <u>our own labors with heaven's blessings as a direct result of our faith,</u> OR from the voluntary charitable acts of assistance from others as they respond to the promptings of God's Spirit. Also as a result of our faith and trust in God's promise to his children, i.e. Matthew 6:25, 29, and 30, "Therefore I say unto you, take no thought for your life.... Consider the lilies of the field, how they grow; they toil not, neither do they spin: and yet I say unto you, that even Solomon in all his glory was not arrayed like one of these. But seek ye first the Kingdom of God, and His righteousness; and all these things shall be added unto you." Also Malachi 3:10, "Bring ye all the tithes into the storehouse,.....and prove me now herewith, saith the Lord of Hosts, if I will not open you the windows of heaven, and pour you out a blessings, that there shall not be room enough to receive it."

The other source is from the anti-Christ who offers <u>money that has been stolen from someone else</u> through legalized plunder. This money is offered firstly in an attempt to make us a party to the theft. (Thou shalt not steal.) Secondly to tempt us to desire or covet other peoples' property. (Thou shalt not covet.) Lastly, it makes us subject to the jurisdiction of the majority of the people who are forced to pay the bill through unjust taxation. This of course is the tool of the anti-Christ to socialize and rob us of our individual rights or independence under the Common Law or God's Law, i.e. Matthew 6:24, "No man can serve two masters: for either he will hate the one, and love the other; or else he will hold to the one, and despise the other. <u>Ye cannot serve God and mammon."</u>

This nation was established as a Christian nation dedicated to faith and trust in Him who made all things. In response to such faith, our nation was made free and became the greatest nation in the world. Through divine intervention, the Constitution was designed and established as the best form of government on earth. That Constitution provided the citizens with the opportunity to live freely without force or coercion from government. That form of government is titled a Constitutional Republic.

Today our nation is ruled by the anti-Christ or heathen principles of democratic socialism. God and moral concepts are outlawed. We function as a nation without faith and as a result, we shall reap the whirlwind, as has every other nation before us who have forsaken God.

It is the duty of every true believer in God's goodness to hold the line of jurisdiction over his own life and the lives of his or her family and over all that God has blessed him or her with, even unto death. God expects it of us and we can therefore give no less.

For those so-called Christian spokespersons who tell us that when Christ said, "Render unto Caesar that which is Caesar's, and unto God that which is God's" He meant for us to give in to all government powers, or submit to all laws established by Caesar. We must say that is certainly a completely false notion. If it were so, Christ would have said, "Render all things unto Caesar, period." No, He left the responsibility of discernment up to us. What is proper for Caesar to do, and what is not. That responsibility is part of our test to prove us, and our faith in Him who made us free.

In our day our Father in Heaven has given us further light on the subject, for He has said, "That law of the land which is constitutional is justifiable before me….whatsoever is more or less than this (Constitutional) cometh of evil." The question is then, IS IT CONSTITUTIONAL.

The burden is ours. We must know the Constitution of the United States and uphold it at all cost. We must labor with all the fervor of our souls to free ourselves from all unconstitutional precepts so evident in our land today. We must sustain all good men and all righteous laws that are in support of that inspired document. We may ignore this responsibility, but we cannot escape its eternal consequences.

Most people realize that we have lost our rights but do not understand how or why it happened. The Constitution is not out moded as we are told. The reason we as a nation are in trouble and turmoil is because we have ignored the vital principles of the Constitution and we have allowed criminals to seize power and authority never authorized by that great document.

We do not know our Constitution. What would happen today if someone ordered the seizing of all copies of the Constitution in the United States? Suppose they were all burned. How many of us could sit down and rewrite it? Probably no one. Because we do not know why it was set up the way it was nor do we know where the principles came from. It certainly is not taught in the government schools.

BANKRUPTCY

Let us take the law of bankruptcy for instance. It is a part of our constitutional system. Let us look at the basic principle behind it. The law of bankruptcy is based upon an ancient biblical law called the Law of Jubilee. The Law of Jubilee provided that if a man went into debt and/or was in servitude to his fellow man because of the debt, or his property had been confiscated as payment for that debt, there was a way out for him. At the end of every forty-nine years all debts were forgiven and all indentured property was returned to the original owners. That way no family or tribe ever lost its inheritance.

Our modern law of bankruptcy is based upon the same principle. Let us suppose that we go into debt beyond our capacity and we find ourselves short financially. We end up with less than we thought we could produce and we cannot meet our obligations. We apply to the bankruptcy court, and we say we have so much money and so many debts and the court asks us to take all our money and divide it equally among all our debtors. We may pay twenty cents or fifty cents on the dollar or what ever we can. We then say, "We need to be forgiven for the rest of the debt" and the court says, "O.K., pay what you can pay and the rest will be forgiven."

The real law that it is based upon is the Law of Redemption. The day will come when we will all go before a bar, with an honorable and just Judge, and we will say we have accumulated so many debts. We will acknowledge that we have hurt that brother's feelings or we have hurt that woman who put her trust in us or we have violated some law or we have done this or that wrong. We have gone back and tried to make amends….we have gone back, apologized, and tried to make everything right that we could, but we came up short because there are some things we just can't make right. Then the Great Judge will say, "Well, my friend I will forgive that because you have made every effort that you could….go and sin no more."

That is what the Law of Redemption is all about. We have it because there was someone, a Savior or Redeemer, who was willing to pay the additional price that we could not.

The Law of Bankruptcy is a divine principle that the Founding Fathers understood. They wrote it into the Constitution to be used righteously; they did not intend for it to be abused as it often is today. That is where it comes from. We must go back and understand those things…we must find the Foundation Stones of common law based upon God's law which gave us the principles to establish the greatest nation on earth. That is why we have been successful—for 200 years we have been the most powerful and beautiful nation on earth.

RIGHT TO FACE OUR ACCUSERS

Another Biblical standard set early in history was "Thou shalt not bear false witness against thy neighbor" and later Christ said, "Speak no evil of any man." This precept was carried on to the time of King Arthur and the Knights of the Round Table whose standards were similar for part of their oath of Chivalry was "listen to no evil of any man unless he is present to defend himself."

This principle of honor has been found in all generations among moral societies and was written into our Constitution. We have the right to face our accusers and the right to a jury trial before our peers where those accusers must also appear so that the accusations and accusers might be weighed in the balance.

In earlier times, if a person was found to be a false accuser, he or she was sentenced to the same penalty as the accused would have received had he been found guilty. Such standards are upheld in a Constitutional Republic and other moral societies.

In the Soviet Union and other nations under the rule of the anti-Christ, stations with direct lines to Communist headquarters are found every few blocks throughout the country. Anyone may use these phones to call in reports on any other person in the country. The accuser is not required to give his or her name or any other means of identification. The accused person is subsequently picked up for questioning and never knows who made the accusations or what the accusations were.

If proper answers are not given by the accused in such cases, imprisonment or even death is the penalty.

Any moral person can see the injustices in such dealings.

We can see the degenerate condition we find our nation in today, for in every town and city in every state in the Union we see signs stating, "CRIME WATCH. If you have any information on child neglect or abuse, drug abuse, wife beating, or any other suspected crime, call such and such a number. It is not necessary to give your name or to identify yourself in any way." Moreover, we as a nation have allowed such perversions of justice without a word of protest.

We have been robed of our birthright because we have lost contact with truth….the Lord says, "Ye shall know the truth and the truth shall make you free."….we are not free, so apparently we must not know the truth. We have lost these basic concepts of government. That is why we must share these simple precepts with others.

These truths are not taught in the schools…"Heaven" forbid that government schools should teach us that we have this much power or that they have usurped that power from us. They do not want us to know they have taken it illegally. Jefferson said that once a liberty is lost to a tyrant, the only way it can be gotten back is by bloodshed. Never has a tyrant relinquished power voluntarily.

UNANIMOUS VOTE

Originally, "the professor" recommended that we should not amend the Constitution without a unanimous vote. This proposal was rejected because some of the men at the Constitutional Convention would not vote for it; they could not get a unanimous vote on the unanimous vote issue. Members were arguing for a simple majority vote for the amendment process. They were starting to sway others who were there. George Washington, who said very little during the entire convention, finally stood up and said, "Gentlemen, let's settle for a two-thirds majority." He saw it was a losing battle to try to get the unanimous vote.

Let us look at this more closely. Let us suppose that three of us form a corporation. We invest our assets, and we all share equally in profits and responsibilities. Then I decide to take a vacation and I return to find that the other two members have changed the contract and have excluded me in their decisions. They have also robbed me of some of my assets. Would I have any redress? In a court of law, I could argue breach of contract because they had not consulted with me and had changed the original agreement outside the scope of their authority and control and without my permission.

Now let us suppose a body of people get together and form a contract that is called the Constitution of the United States. Two-thirds of them, after the original agreement is made, decide to change the contract. Could they legally do so without the consent of all concerned? The answer is obviously no. that is why "the professor" told the Founding Fathers that they should require a unanimous vote on the amendment process. Do you think they could have changed the Constitution had a unanimous vote been required? No. they could not.

VIOLATION OF OATH OF OFFICE

The second article which was to be added to the Constitution, and which was left out because they could not get a unanimous vote on it, was the death penalty for anyone who violated his oath of office. How many believe that there would be elected or appointed representatives of the people violating their oath of office if they knew that there was a death penalty assigned to such violations? No sir!

IMMIGRATION

The problem is this: we now have a totalitarian form of government over us, which has totally changed our form of government. It has also opened the gates of our land to any type of intrusion. We have an illegal influx of over ten million people into our country who have entered without the safeguard of the proper immigration process.

Now I am not opposed to individuals coming into our country. My parents were immigrants. My father was in the German merchant marines for four years having joined when he was fourteen years old. When he got off the ship in New York and asked to be immigrated, he had already sailed around the world twice. He worked his way across the United States to St. Louis where he met my mother who had preceded him here by six months. She was working as a servant girl in the home of a wealthy family. He married her and they moved to Indiana, Illinois, and then to Wisconsin where I was born.

All during the time when I was small, I remember my parents' going to city hall and taking a study course in preparation for their receiving their citizenship. They would come home and tell us the wonderful things they were learning about America. They would say, "We could not do this thing in the old country....look how free we are." They would explain to us many of these basic principles. That is where I learned to appreciate this great land.

I remember one Saturday when I was about five years old. That day my parents came home with the tears streaming down their cheeks to tell us that they had received their papers. "We are American citizens and we will never speak anything again but English because we are Americans." They told my two brothers and me to fight always for this land because this was the greatest land on earth.

I do not mind people's coming into our country. I am all for it because there is a certain process that made this nation great. Those that had the courage and stamina to leave their homelands, come to this country, and carve out a new nation were the greatest people on earth. They came here to work for themselves and build a land of their own. They did not come over here to be a drag on society. They did not come over here to bleed our nation dry by taking from those who produce and are successful.

Today our country is being overrun purposely by aliens. They cross our borders from the south, and they come in by boat from Cuba and the Far East in uncontrolled numbers to swell our unemployment and welfare rolls. They demand free education, free food, and free housing, all of which is far beyond the productive taxpayers' capacity to provide!

WASHINGTON'S VISION

George Washington as leader of our nation knelt in prayer many times. One time, when at Valley Forge, being especially concerned about discouraging conditions, he knelt to appeal to Heaven for guidance. After praying, he went back into his quarters and sat down at the table to consider the activities of the next day. Presently the room lit up as if it were noonday. He looked up and saw an angel standing before him.

How many of you have ever read an account of the vision that he had?[3] It was a vision concerning the history or future of America. General McClelland had a similar vision during the War Between the States.

He saw that there would be three great tribulations or trials that would come upon America. The first one was the war in which he was fighting, the Revolutionary War. He saw that the colonists would win, and it gave him the courage to go on. The lord knew that he needed that help, so he showed him this vision to give him the strength to continue. Then Washington saw that there would be another great trial upon the land that would be the dividing of the nation, the North against the South. He saw that that rupture would be mended and that the feelings would be healed and brother would join hands with brother again.

THE THIRD AND GREATEST PERIL

In the last scene shown to Washington, he saw dark clouds rolling in all over our country from all the nations of the earth. Armed men were coming in from all directions from all the other nations. They came by land and by sea causing great upheavals and insurrections. Every major city, town, and village in America was inflamed with insurrection.

America sank to such a weakened condition that it looked as if there were nothing more we could do to defend ourselves. Washington saw that in this state of hopelessness, other great nations would come in expecting to take over our country because we were so weak and divided. Washington said it looked as if the fragments of the American Army were so disorganized and demoralized that they

---

3   See Annex B, "The Vision of George Washington" and Annex C, "America's Future (The Dream of General McClelland)"

could hardly defend themselves. They were driven into retreat with their backs against the Rocky Mountains.

At the point when it looked as if there was absolutely no hope, they saw a light shining in the heavens, brighter than ten thousands suns. Legions of bright spirits came down from the heavens, drove from this land the enemies of liberty, and established the standard of freedom forever and forever.

That is a wonderful promise.

REMNANT

Isn't it a wonderful promise to know that, in spite of all the evil men design, in spite of the tyrants of the world who have robbed us of our birthright, in spite of all the efforts on the part of phony government that God is still at the helm? Though power-hungry men have shaken the very foundation of our nation and have robbed us of every God-given right that we have, the torch of our enemies will only cleanse and humble our land.

When that humbling period is over, those who are left will understand these precepts of government. Those who are left will recognize that there is one Sovereign and only one. Those people will be spared in the last hour, God will come and set up His Kingdom under these precepts, and it will reign forever and forever.

I will be glad when phony government officials who presume to preside over us are gone. I will be glad when the tyrants are swept from our land. I will be glad when the abortions have ceased and the blood of the one and one half million children who are murdered each year no longer cries up from the soil to our Father in Heaven for vengeance. I will be glad when the homosexuals are gone and can no longer teach and pervert our youth. I will be glad when Sodom and Gomorrah are wiped clean. I will be glad when men again raise their eyes to heaven and recognize that God is the ruler of all the world and all the creations and eternities. When we see that day, we will see this land of America delivered as Israel of old was delivered by His hand.

There will not be many people here to fight the battle because it shall be as it was when Gideon went to fight the armies of the enemies of Israel. The lord said, "Don't take a large number of people with you because then you won't see My hand in it. Go down and get just a handful of men. Let the enemy outnumber you fifty or one hundred to one; then you will see the delivering arm of the God of Liberty."

Father in Heaven does not need many people. I am not discouraged that there are just a few patriots, are you? It is a wonderful promise we have and we should ask the Lord to bless us to understand the responsibility that goes with that promise….to know the principles upon which this nation was founded so that we can help Heavenly Father re-establish it in righteousness when the opportunity comes.

Let us study and prepare ourselves that we will not be tyrants. Let us learn His ways that we will not deprive another man of his rights because we will not agree with his religion or his ideas. Let us understand that every man has his free agency under God and is directly responsible to Him. We must come to understand these precepts clearly, so our country can be free again.

If we do not understand them, we are not going to live to see that day when the Constitution is re-established in its perfect form. When that day comes, it is going to have these provisions also: the death penalty for those who violate their oath of office and the requirement of a unanimous vote for any changes to be made to the Constitution. Those principles along with others will be written into a perfect Constitution because this time Heavenly Father Himself will oversee and direct us.

A Summary

In short summary we see that all the safeguards and the checks against totalitarian government have been removed and destroyed by careful behind-the-scenes planning over the years.

Government no longer functions under the limited power of delegated authority of the individual citizens.

No longer are taxes levied equally; today the productive citizens support not only unbridled government but all nonproductive citizens as well. In addition, those who protest or try to teach the truth of just taxation are harassed, persecuted, imprisoned, and even killed by agents of this alien government.

The gold and silver currency of the Constitution has been replaced with unbacked bogus paper money of the privately owned Federal Reserve Corporation owned and controlled by the world banking interests. The debt and interest on this debt to the Federal Reserve System is called our National Debt. The reason the illegal income tax was created was to bilk our children and us for the next 5 generations for payment of this illegal interest.

The right to keep and bear arms is slowly being eroded away by that same government we hired to help us protect ourselves from the criminal element. Today the government-controlled courts protect the criminal and at every opportunity attempt to deprive the law-abiding citizens of the right and means of protecting themselves and opposing tyranny in government.

The Congress has relinquished its right and duty to make laws and declare war. The Executive Branch has usurped that power.

The states have failed to maintain a standing militia while the Federal Government has taken control of the state militia by Federalizing a National Guard and through the draft has forced all our other able-bodied citizens, of the various states, to serve in an unconstitutional Federal Standing Army. The Founding Fathers understood that such an Army could be used as a National Police Force to control the citizenry were they to attempt to throw off the chains of tyranny. The Executive Branch has usurped the responsibility of Congress and commits our youth to fight in undeclared no-win wars, while "American" businesses trade with and give aid and comfort to the very enemies that are killing our boys.

The safeguard of the separation of powers has been by-passed and all three powers are now consolidated into the Executive Branch, i.e. OSHA, IRS, EPA, HEW, etc. Thus, totalitarian power is in the hands of a few unelected officials.

The education of our children has been taken over by a federally controlled tax financed education system. Perverts are allowed to teach in these schools with equal or more recognition than moral educators do. The safeguards of a Constitutional Republic are carefully excluded from the curriculum so a new generation will grow up with no understanding as to the dangers of a socialistic society. The proven values of Biblical morality are forbidden while the age old God-less, materialistic humanism of the anti-Christ is forced upon the innocent, unsuspecting youth of our nation as though it were some newly discovered revelation of truth. These vast changes in the education standards have resulted in the moral decay of our society.

As the ultimate check against bad laws, the citizens as members of a jury have the duty to judge the morality of the law as well as the fact of guilt of the accused. This right and the use of the Constitution as a defense have been denied us by corrupt judges in nearly every court in the land.

Lastly, the unconstitutional ruling by the Supreme Court in 1967, which changed the voting areas in the Senate districts, has deprived the less populated areas of the right to representation.

THE ULTIMATE CONSEQUENCES

These vast changes have indeed converted our form of government into a socialistic Democracy, and as a result, we must pay the price of such changes—for eventually every Democracy has collapsed because of its own corruption. The "leaders" of such a government cannot forever continue to increase the tax burden on the few productive citizens to satisfy the clamoring of the nonproductive mobs; eventually the money runs out and there are still clamorers standing at the trough for their handout. When none is forthcoming, they feel justified in going to the streets to "get what's coming to them". The ultimate result then is anarchy and total collapse of society.

This then is our future, but it really is not as bleak as it looks, for there are many things we can do to prepare to survive such a calamity.

SPIRITUAL PREPARATION

<u>THE FIRST AND MOST IMPORTANT THING IS GETTING CLOSE TO OUR FATHER IN HEAVEN BY KEEPING HIS LAWS AND COMMANDMENTS.</u> All other preparations are of little use if this is not first accomplished, for the reason we are facing this dilemma is that we as a nation have forgotten Him and have failed to make His laws our laws.

Then, in addition to our spiritual preparation, we should physically prepare for defense against the planned destruction and enslavement of our country by organizing ourselves into independent civil defense teams.

When I retired from the Service in 1969 and settled in Utah, we successfully organized Salt Lake County and surrounding counties into independent civil defense teams. Because of our experiences in this endeavor, I can suggest some steps to follow:

INDEPENDENT CIVIL DEFENSE TEAMS

First, choose a geographical location with such features as streams, an elevation, or a man-made wall which would tend to mark off that particular area as a neighborhood. (See Chart #4) Choose one person as a commander to be responsible for all the civil defense activities in that area. Then choose five Junior Commanders, each of whom would have a team working under his direction. The members of each of these teams would concentrate on their team's particular job. One team would be in charge of food and water storage; another medical aid; a third, communications; a fourth, security; and fifth, countermeasures.

FOOD AND WATER

We will first need to have food in storage sufficient for our need for one year, and we will need water. The lack of water is one of the main causes of panic in cases of emergency. In Utah, there are artesian wells and springs bubbling in many locations of Salt Lake City and surrounding counties.

We went to the Safety Commissioner and County Engineers and secured maps on which we plotted these wells and springs. Each neighborhood leader received a record of the water sources.

They then assigned men with pickup trucks and fifty-five gallon drums or stainless steel milk tankers to be ready in case of emergency such as riots or earthquakes, etc. their plan was to go to the water sources, fill up their trucks, and deliver water door-to-door on a regularly scheduled basis. They were to determine beforehand the amounts necessary for survival. Man cannot survive long without water!

The reason that there is going to be insurrection in this country is that it is hoped by our enemies that once everything is chaotic, the government can declare martial law and impose its jurisdiction over all aspects of our lives and align us with a one world totalitarian government under the anti-Christ. Their jurisdiction can extend to forcing us to take the Mark of the Beast. If there is no chaos or insurrection in your area, there will be no excuse for the imposition of martial law. Independent civil defense preparation will help stabilize your area beforehand and avert the panic our enemies hope to create.

MEDICAL TEAMS

You are also going to need access to medical aid. Choose a nurse, doctor, paramedic, or some other person who has had training in the medical profession. In Utah, we had Red Cross personnel come in and train team members that wanted to be trained in rendering emergency medical aid. These people prepared a central location within their neighborhood or communities to be used as a clearinghouse (for storage of medical supplies) and an evacuation station where most medical problems could be handled. This is the way to control the situation, and help keep panic down.

COMMUNICATION AND SECURITY

The third and fourth areas are communication and security. These areas are interrelated and of paramount importance. How many of us have children in public schools? It is a usual policy of the school, in times of emergency, for all children to be sent to the auditorium to remain there awaiting further governmental instructions. Kenneth Goff, who was a Communist agent in this country for seventeen years, testified before the American Congress that our enemies plan to take advantage of this policy to hold the children hostages in order to force the parents to conform. (The busing of children over long distances serves the purposes of behind-the-scenes planners.)

According to Mr. Goff, rioters would create civil disturbances on one side of town at ten in the morning and on the other side of town at one or two o'clock in the afternoon. The services of all the police and their auxiliaries would be required to quell the riots. While the police are thus occupied, the insurrectionists would be able to take over the schools and communication systems and blackmail the parents into submission.

Those of you who were in Vietnam will remember the election times in 1968 when children of the village chiefs and other leaders were kidnapped. They were told that if they would not conform and take directions from the Communists, they would never see their children again. Pieces of the children of those who disobeyed were sent home in bags. Terrorists control the public the world over that way! Criminal minds of men like Robert Williams (RAM), Stokely Charmichael, Rap Brown, Jerry Rubins and hundreds of other trained revolutionaries are planning the same terrorist activities for our country.

Now stop and think what would happen if a riot occurred in your area and your children were in school on the other side of town? What would you do? Suddenly mother realizes the danger. She jumps into the family car and speeds across town, or tries to do so. At the same time, thousands of other mothers are doing the same thing. What do you? think the traffic would be like? How far do you think you would get? The ensuing panic would cause utter chaos giving the government the excuse they want to impose martial law.

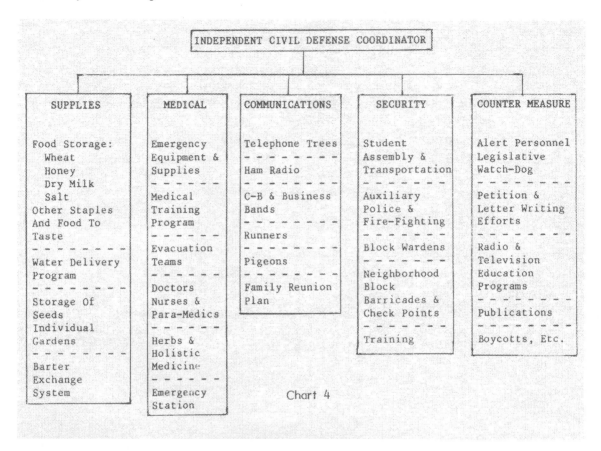

Chart 4

In Utah, by way of preventing such events, we took the team leaders and our other trained personnel who lived or worked closest to the school and assigned them to go to that school and get the children out. They were to place them in a secure area controlled by the citizens themselves. Then, using their own communication system prepared beforehand, they were to contact all the other groups and have them send one representative plus guards with bus or van from each neighborhood. They would pick up the children from their assigned areas and deliver them home to their parents.

In answer to a question made from the audience during our speaking tours, I will say that we contacted school administrators apprising them of our plans. We already had the sanction of the Safety Commissioner, and we had cleared our security forces with the Chief of Police who understood the problem. At our request, our men were trained as auxiliary police officers. They took the same exams, both mental and physical, that regular police officers take plus all the other kinds of tests for competence that are required of full time police officers. We took the full training course.

We also bought our own uniforms, our own guns, badges, and other equipment. We served four hours per week as auxiliary police officers at no cost to the local government. They appreciated our services as they had a heavy workload. In times of emergency, we were already deputized to maintain law and order in our areas and to make arrests when necessary. We were available to protect our own children should the need arise. These experiences taught us the value of a citizen's militia.

COUNTERMEASURE

The activities of the countermeasure team are the last to be discussed. I will relate to you some of our experiences with this team. When I first arrived in Utah, an insurrection newspaper was engaged in trying to stir up civil unrest. By means of our telephone tree, we contacted the eighty-five firms who were advertising in this paper thereby causing all but two of them to withdraw their advertising. This aim was accomplished within a day and a half. The newspaper went broke.

The telephone tree, our alert system, works like this: the person starting the operation makes five local calls plus one long-distance call. Each person thus contacted then makes five local calls and one long-distance call. In a very short time, it is possible to alert all the people involved in this civil defense organization. In this case we asked three hundred people to call the advertisers the first morning, three hundred that afternoon, and three hundred the next morning. Nine hundred callers contacted these advertisers and by noon of the second day, there remained only two advertisers still willing to do business with this newspaper.

Another time a friend of mine, Kaylan Harper, was picked up in Laramie, Wyoming, for selling Bibles door-to-door. In Wyoming, it is against the Green River Ordinance to sell anything door-to-door. In passing this un-Constitutional ordinance, the local people overrode a congressional enactment of years back making it illegal to interfere with the sale of the Bible in America, and the U.S. Constitution, which states no laws shall be passed interfering with the right of contract.

Kaylan was thrown into jail and ordered to either pay a hundred dollar fine or serve thirty days. Kaylan told them he did not have one hundred dollars to pay and would not pay it if he did because his rights were being violated. He is a member of our telephone tree, so he called me in Montana to apprise me of his predicament. I called Joye Wyatt in Utah and we both called people all over the country. All of us began calling the Governor, the Secretary of State, the County Attorney, the County Sheriff, the Police Chief, and the Judge in Wyoming in addition to our own Senators from our home states. They all received dozens of phone calls within about two hours. They must have felt as if they were being watched by the whole world.

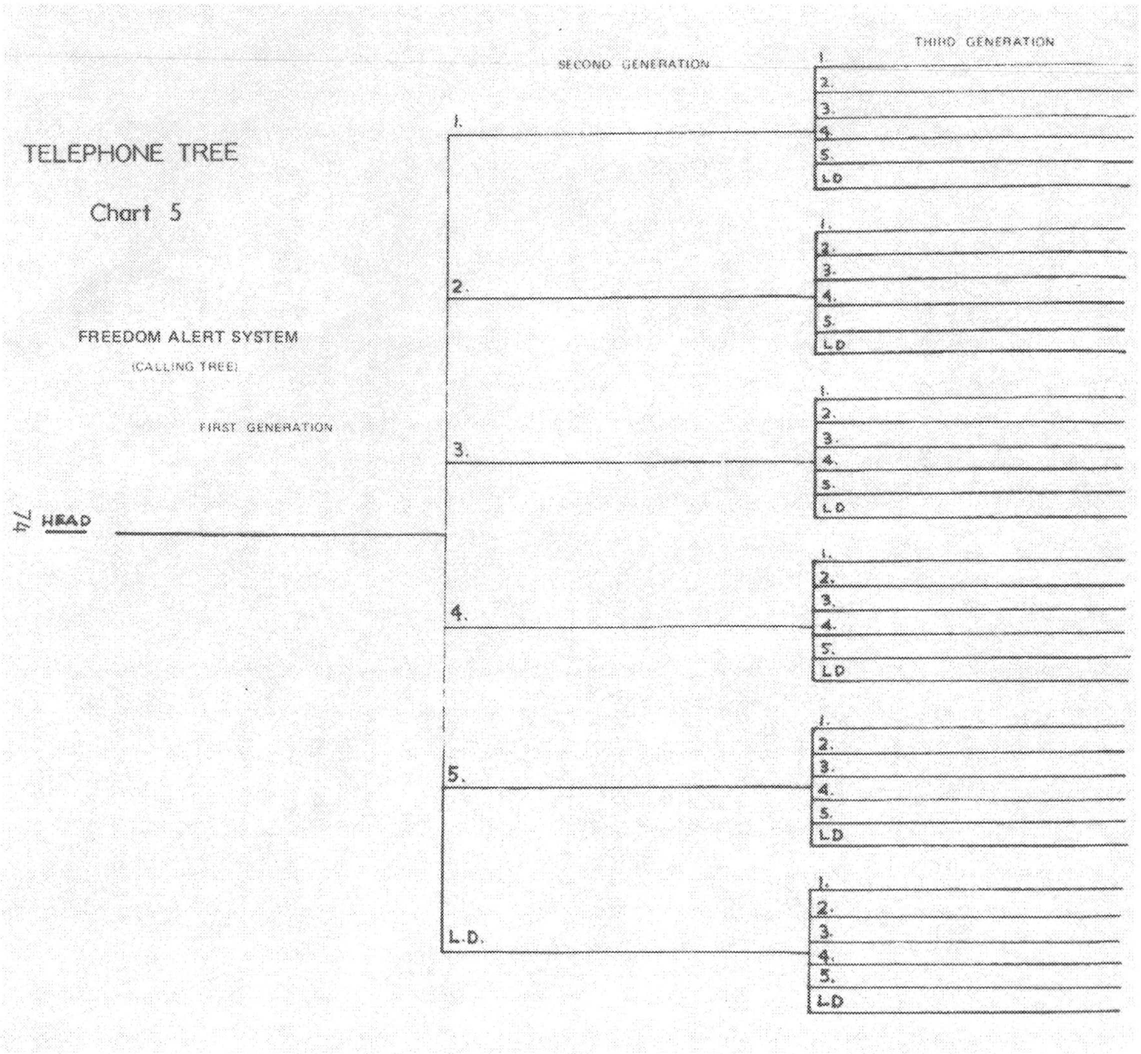

TELEPHONE TREE

Chart 5

FREEDOM ALERT SYSTEM

(CALLING TREE)

FIRST GENERATION

SECOND GENERATION

THIRD GENERATION

HEAD

At nine that morning the Judge had my friend in Court for arraignment. He asked Kaylan which he was going to do, pay the fine or spend thirty days in jail. Kaylan replied that he would do neither.

At three o'clock that afternoon, Kaylan was called back to Court together with the arresting officer, a woman. The Judge said to the officer, "Did you actually see him selling those Bibles?"

The officer replied, "Well, no, I did not, but he came away from the door with his brief case and I asked him what he was doing and he said…"

At this point the Judge broke in with, "Don't tell me what he said. Did you actually see him selling those Bibles?"

"No," replied the officer.

"Case dismissed," snapped the Judge.

You can see that we can help one another with the telephone tree, and the countermeasure team is all about helping one another.

We can do something to keep unjust practices out of our own areas even though the rest of the nation allows them in their areas. There will be places that will not suffer injustice. Isaiah said that if you did not want to take up your swords against your neighbor, you had better get up into the

mountains. That means that in the mountains we are not going to take up swords against one another. We are even going to have law and order, Constitutional law and order.

Isaiah said that in the last days the wicked would destroy the wicked. If we are down there in the streets of the big cities shooting the wicked, who are we? Where do we want to be? Do we want to be in the big cities when the insurrection begins? Are we going to stay and be a part of the destruction that is going on? Insurrectionists will not get to every mountain valley until they are very humble because they will have to climb over the mountains and walk every step of the way.

THE AMERICAN DREAM WILL PREVAIL

If they come, weary and humbled with their hats in their hands, we will gladly share everything we have with them. We hope for this kind of country. That is the kind of country I was raised in. When I was a kid in Wisconsin, if our neighbor's barn burned down, we all helped to build him another barn. If our family needed something, our neighbors came over and helped us. We did not have to ask and we did not have to stand in some welfare line; we knew one another's hearts and we cared.

Many have lost confidence in the American Dream. Some do not believe it can still work. We are going to make it work in the tops of the mountains....of that you can be sure. If you cannot find enough Americans to make it work where you live, then get out and go to a place where you can, and may God bless you not to be afraid.

"FEAR NOT, I AM WITH THEE"

I know what fear is, for when I first arrived in Vietnam, I was afraid. I knelt by my bed that first night as I do each day and I asked my Father in Heaven to please help me not to be afraid. I soon fell asleep and was awakened about three in the morning by the sound of a beautiful hymn ringing in my heart. It was the third verse of a hymn called "How Firm a Foundation" which goes like this:

"Fear not I am with thee,
Oh, be not dismayed
For I am thy God
And will still give thee aid
I'll strengthen thee, help thee
And cause thee to stand,
Upheld by my righteous omnipotent hand."

During my stay in Vietnam, I flew 253 aerial observer missions. I fought all night and into the next day of the "TET" offensive of '68. I have often seen tracer bullets rise from the ground to meet us in the air, each time a sweet peace came over me, and the words of that song rang out in my heart. What a wonderful thing the Gospel is, and what hope we have in His promises to us.

May we never forget that God has labored to bring about a free America, and with His help that Dream shall never die. This is my conviction in the Holy Name of Jesus Christ, Amen.

Points to Ponder

The average age of the world's great civilizations has been 200 years. These nations progressed through this sequence:

From bondage to spiritual faith
From spiritual faith to great courage
From great courage to liberty
From liberty to abundance
From abundance to selfishness
From selfishness to complacency
From complacency to apathy
From apathy to dependency
From dependency back again to bondage

The United States has reached the 200-year mark. This cycle is not inevitable – It all depends on you!

Supplementary Material

NOTES ON THE NEIGHBORHOOD EMERGENCY TEAMS

1. SKILLS: Each and everyone has at least one talent that can be used should an emergency occur in his or her neighborhood—medical aid, repairs of any nature, firefighting, communications, water treatment, child care, and many others.

2. COMMUNICATIONS: An important consideration is to maintain communication with family members. If you do not have transmitter/receiver equipment, a more practical means of communication may be the use of homing pigeons. Within your community, you can use lights (at night), flags, runners, bicycle, motorbike, or other means.

3. LIGHTING: A generator using diesel or white gasoline can power a small lighting system as well as your communications equipment. Coal oil lamps with a 1" wick will burn 45 hours on a quart of fuel; at 5 hours per day, it will burn 10 gallons of fuel per year. Flashlights will burn 6 to 7 hours on new batteries. Candles: ¾ " diameter, 4" high will burn 2 hours and 20 minutes; 7/8" diameter, 4" high will burn 5 hours; 2" diameter, 9" high will burn 63 hours.

4. FUEL: Needed for emergency vehicles (ambulance, fire trucks, communications), heating, cooking. Coal oil, kerosene, diesel, white gas, and/or coal should be stored underground. Wood, charcoal, and rolled newspaper should also be stored for fuel.

5. COOKING AND HEATING: A wood and coal stove with oven is the best to have. Be sure you have stovepipe on hand even if only a home-fabricated stove is used. A hanging fireplace can be used for cooking as well as heating. A "Dutch Oven" (cast iron pot with lid) can be used right on the coals. You can cook in a charcoal stove or over an open pit in your backyard.

6. FIRST AID: Each family should be knowledgeable of how to STOP BLEEDING, CLEAR BREATHING PASSAGES, TREAT FRACTURES AND BURNS, PREVENT SHOCK, and make a patient comfortable. At least one member of each family should be knowledgeable of MINOR OPERATION techniques and the delivery of a baby.

7. SANITATION: Improper disposal of human waste can cause epidemics of typhoid,

dysentery, and diarrhea. Use a covered pail to store human waste until it is buried. Bury human waste and garbage 12" to 24" below the surface away from water sources. DO NOT flush toilet should your water supply be cut off. Water can be used for cooking or drinking. Some items which should be kept on hand include paper plates, cups, napkins, towels; soap, toilet tissue, sanitary napkins, diapers; newspapers, grocery bags, insect spray, tools (turning off service line water valve); chlorine solution (Clorox), washboard, garbage can (20 gallon size), waste can (10 gallon size), and a shovel (to bury the garbage and wastes).

8. STORAGE: Store only those items YOUR family will use in the one or two year period. Plan your storage. Consider the variety of items you will require besides food. List these items in a column. Beside these items list the 12 months of the year and your needs for each month. Then add a total column.

9. WATER: Water is of PRIME importance. One can survive on water alone for over a month. It can be stored in any plastic, glass or metal container. If after a long period of time water becomes odorous it may still be useable. In case local water supplies are cut off, you should know where the main shut-off valve is located leading into your house. All the water in the house plumbing system can be used—hot water heater, water softener, flush box and pipes. Sediment in the hot water heater should be drained out monthly. Water can be purified with tablets (as prescribed on the bottle), with iodine (2 or 3 drops per quart), with sodium hypochlorite (Clorox) (4-10 drops per gallon—insure that you can taste the chlorine), or boil water and let stand 30 minutes. You can increase the supply of water in your home by installing collapsible rubber tanks in your attic and connecting with your water supply using flexible piping. Conserve your water!

10. FOOD: One item that should be in every food storage plan is Vitamin C tablets. Vitamin C will not store in the BODY, but it will in the BOTTLE. It is needed to maintain good health. It is found in tomato juice and paprika. Date all the food that you store, and keep a record of all you store against that which you require. Minimum daily requirements are 700 calories per day to EXIST, or about 5000 calories per week. The basic, minimum existence diet should include: WHEAT (300 lbs. per person per year); POWDERED MILK (100 lbs. per person per year); HONEY (55-75 lbs. per person per year) or SUGAR (100 lbs. per person per year); SALT (5 lbs. per person per year). These four basic foods will store almost indefinitely if stored properly—35 to 65 degrees F., out of the sun and dust, and away from any moisture. All other foods are stored the same but must be rotated. Keep in mind that wheat, peas, beans, and some seeds can be sprouted to increase your food supply and food value.

11. POWER FAILURE: Have you thought what you should do if the power fails? Your 'frige, freezer, and stove could be cut off. What to do with the food? Eat or bottle perishable foods first. Cook or smoke meats, or soak in a salt brine. Bread can be eaten even if moldy. Sour milk is drinkable. Cut the rotten spots out of the fruits and vegetables and eat them. Fido's food is edible also. Remember to open only those foods you need since you have no means to store leftovers.

12. FIREFIGHTING: Keep a garden hose with nozzle in kitchen or where hose can be

connected. Have a couple of buckets handy to fight fires. You should have at least one good fire extinguisher on hand to fight any kind of fire.

13. DAMAGE REPAIR: Windows blown out? Keep a supply of plywood on hand, or use Plexiglas, acetate or plastic to cover windows. You will need tools to repair—hammer, saw, screwdriver, pliers, etc., also a supply of nails, screws, bolts, etc.

SUPPLEMENTARY MATERIAL

FOOD STORAGE PROGRAM

Amounts for 5 Persons per year storage

Chart 6

ITEMS	AMOUNTS	PERSONAL INVENTORY			NEED		
		APR	AUG	DEC	APR	AUG	DEC
BAKING POWDER	6 CANS						
BEANS, DRIED	100 LBS						
FRUIT, CANS OR QUARTS APPLE SAUCE, TOMATOES, PEACHES, APRICOTS, PINEAPPLE, GRAPEFRUIT (OTHERS DO NOT STORE WELL)	365 CANS						
HONEY (55 LBS)	10 CANS						
JELLO	4-6 CASES						
JUICES PINEAPPLE, GRAPE, GRAPEFRUIT, TOMATO (THESE STORE BEST)	208 CANS						
MARGARINE	90 LBS						
MEAT CANNED BEEF, TUNA, SPAM, CHIPPED BEEF, ETC.	250 CANS						
MILK, EVAPORATED, POWDERED	4 CASES 48 CARTONS						
POTATOES, DRIED	12 CANS						
SALT, IODIZED	12 PKGS						
SHORTENING, 3 LBS	12 CANS						
SODA	12 PKGS						
SOUP	730 CANS						
SUGAR	200 LBS						
VEGETABLES CORN NIBLETS, PEAS, CREAM CORN (OTHERS DO NOT STORE WELL)	730 CANS						
WHEAT	25 BU						
YEAST	8 PKGS						
BLEACH	4 GAL						
CANDLES	365						
MATCHES	12 BOXES						
SHEETS, LARGE	14						
SOAP, HAND, POWDERED	75 BARS 25 PKGS						
TOILET TISSUE	200 ROLLS						
VITAMIN C	1825 PILLS						
WATER	365 QTS						
COAL (IF YOU HAVE A FIREPLACE OR STOVE TO BURN IT,)	1 TON (SUGGESTED)						

Annex A

The Unknown Who Swayed the Signers
of the Declaration of Independence

Faced with the death penalty for high treason, courageous men debated long before they picked up the quill pen to sign the parchment that declared the independence of the colonies from the mother country on July 4, 1776. For many hours, they had debated in the State House at Philadelphia, with the lower chamber doors locked and a guard posted.

According to Jefferson, it was late in the afternoon before the delegates gathered their courage to the sticking point. The talk was about axes, scaffolds, and the gibbet, when suddenly a strong, bold voice sounded—"Gibbet! They may stretch our necks on all the gibbets in the land; they may turn every rock into a scaffold; every tree into a gallows; every home into a grave, and yet the words of that parchment can never die! They may pour our blood on a thousand scaffolds, and yet from every drop that dyes the axe a new champion of freedom will spring into birth! The British King may blot out the stars of God from the sky, but he cannot blot out His words written on that parchment there. The works of God may perish: his words never!

"The words of this declaration will live in the world long after our bones are dust. To the mechanic in his workshop they will speak hope: to the slave in the mines freedom: but to the coward kings, these words will speak in tones of warning they cannot choose but hear.

"Sign that parchment! Sign, if the next moment the gibbet's rope is about your neck! Sign, if the next minute this hall rings with the clash of falling axes! Sign, by all your hopes in life or death, as men, as husbands, as fathers, brothers, sign your names to the parchment, or be accursed forever! Sign, and not only for yourselves, but for all ages, for that parchment will be the textbook of freedom, the bible of the rights of man forever.

"Nay, do not start and whisper with surprise! It is truth; your own hearts witness it: God proclaims it. Look at this strange band of exiles and outcasts, suddenly transformed into a people; a handful of men, weak in arms, but mighty in God-like faith; nay, look at your recent achievements, your Bunker Hill, your Lexington, and then tell me, if you can, that God has not given America to be free!

"It is not given to our poor human intellect to climb to the skies, and to pierce the Council of the Almighty One. But methinks I stand among the awful clouds which veil the brightness of Jehovah's throne.

"Methinks I see the recording Angel come trembling up to the throne and speak his dread message. 'Father, the old world is baptized in blood. Father, look with one glance of Thine eternal

53

eye, and behold evermore that terrible sight, man trodden beneath the oppressor's feet, nations lost in blood, murder, and superstition, walking hand in hand over the graves of the victims, and not a single voice of hope to man!"

"He stands there, the Angel, trembling with the record of human guilt. But hark! The voice of God speaks from out the awful cloud: 'let there be light again! Tell my people, the poor and oppressed, to go out from the old world, from oppression and blood, and build My altar in the new.'

"As I live, my friends, I believe that to be His voice! Yes, were my soul trembling on the verge of eternity, were this hand freezing in death, were this voice choking in the last struggle, I would still, with the last impulse of that soul, with the last wave of that hand, with the last gasp of that voice, implore you to remember this truth—God has given America to be free!

"Yes, as I sank into the gloomy shadows of the grave, with my last faint whisper I would beg you to sign that parchment for the sake of those millions whose very breath is now hushed in intense expectation as they look up to you for the awful words: 'You are free.'"

The unknown speaker fell exhausted into his seat. The delegates, carried away by his enthusiasm, rushed forward. John Hancock scarcely had time to pen his bold signature before the quill was grasped by another. It was done.

The delegates turned to express their gratitude to the unknown speaker for his eloquent words. He was not there.

Who was this strange man, who seemed to speak with a divine authority, whose solemn words gave courage to the doubters and sealed the destiny of the new nation?

His name is not recorded; none of those present knew him; or if they did, not one acknowledged the acquaintance.

How he had entered into the locked and guarded room is not told, nor is there any record of the manner of his departure.

(Taken from the book: The Secret Destiny of America by Manly P. Hall)

Annex B

The Vision of George Washington

The vision of George Washington has been printed and reprinted many times—in books, magazines and in pamphlet form. It was originally published by Wesley Bradshaw. The following account is taken from a reprint published in the <u>National Tribune,</u> Volume 4, No. 12, December 1880.

The last time I ever saw Anthony Sherman was on the fourth of July, 1859, in Independence Square. He was then ninety-nine years old and becoming very feeble. But though so old, his dimming eyes rekindled as he gazed upon Independence Hall which he had come to look upon once more before he was gathered home.

"Let us go into the hall," he said. "I want to tell you an incident of Washington's life—one which no one alive knows of except myself; and, if you live, you will before long see it verified. Mark the prediction. You will see it verified.

"From the opening of the Revolution we experienced all phases of fortune, now good and now ill, one time victorious, and another conquered. The darkest period we had, I think, was when Washington, after several reverses, retreated to Valley Forge where he resolved to pass the winter of '77. Ah! I have often seen the tears coursing down our dear old commander's careworn cheeks, as he would be conversing with a confidential officer about the condition of his poor soldiers. You have doubtless heard the story of Washington going to the thicket to pray. Well, it was not only true, but he used often to pray in secret for aid and comfort from God, the interposition of whose Divine Providence brought us safely through those dark days of tribulation. One day, I remember it well, the chilly winds whistled through the leafless trees, though the sky was cloudless and the sun shone brightly, he remained in his quarters nearly all the afternoon alone. When he came out, I noticed that his face was a shade paler than usual, and there seemed to be something on his mind of more than ordinary importance. Returning just after dusk, he dispatched an orderly to the quarters of the officer I mention who was presently in attendance. After a preliminary conversation of about a half hour, Washington, gazing upon his companion with that strange look of dignity that he alone could command, said to the latter:

"'I do not know whether it is owing to the anxiety of my mind, or what, but this afternoon as I was sitting at this very table engaged in preparing a dispatch, something in the apartment seemed to disturb me. Looking up, I beheld standing opposite to me a singularly beautiful female. So astonished was I, for I had given strict orders not to be disturbed, that it was some moments before I found language to inquire the cause of her presence. A second, a third, and even a fourth time, did I repeat my question, but received no answer from my mysterious visitor except a slight rising of the eyes. By this time, I felt strange sensations spreading through me. I would have risen, but the riveted gaze of the being before me rendered volition impossible. I essayed once more to address her, but my tongue had become powerless. Even thought itself suddenly became paralyzed. A new influence, mysterious, potent, irresistible, took possession of me. All I could do was to gaze steadily, vacantly, at my unknown visitant. Gradually the surrounding atmosphere seemed as though becoming filled with sensations, and grew luminous. Everything about me seemed to rarefy, the mysterious visitor herself becoming more airy, and yet more distinct to my sight than before. I now began to feel as one dying, or rather to experience the sensations that I have sometimes imagined accompany dissolution. I did not think, I did not reason, I did not move, all were alike impossible. I was only conscious of gazing fixedly, vacantly, at my companion.

"Presently I heard a voice saying, 'Son of the Republic, look and learn.' While at the same time, my visitor extended her arm eastwardly. I now beheld a heavy white vapor at some distance, rising fold upon fold. This gradually dissipated, and I looked upon a strange scene. Before me, lay spread out in one vast plain all the countries of the world, Europe, Asia, Africa and America. I saw rolling and tossing between Europe and America the billows of the Atlantic and between Asia and America lay the Pacific. 'Son of the Republic,' said the same mysterious voice as before, 'look and learn.' At that moment, I beheld a dark shadowy being like an angel standing or rather floating in mid-air between Europe and America. Dipping water out of the ocean in the hollow of each hand, he sprinkled some upon America with his right hand while with his left hand he cast some on Europe. Immediately a dark cloud rose from these countries and joined in mid-ocean. For a while it remained stationary and then moved slowly westward until it enveloped America in its murky folds. Sharp flashes of lightning gleamed through it at intervals, and I heard the smothered groans and cries of the American people. A second time the angel dipped water from the ocean, and sprinkled it as before. The dark cloud was then drawn back to the ocean in whose heaving billows it sank from view. A third time I heard the mysterious voice saying, 'Son of the Republic, look and learn.' I cast my eyes upon America and beheld villages and towns and cities springing up, one after another until the whole land from the Atlantic to the Pacific was dotted with them. Again, I heard the mysterious voice say, 'Son of the Republic, the end of the century cometh, look and learn.'

"'At this the dark, shadowy angel turned his face southward, and from Africa I saw an ill-omened specter approach our land. It flitted slowly and heavily over every town and city of the latter. The inhabitants presently set themselves in battle array against each other. As I continued looking, I saw a bright angel, on whose brow rested a crown of light on which was traced the word 'union,' bearing the American flag, which he placed between the divided nation and said, 'Remember ye are brethren.' Instantly the inhabitants, casting from them their weapons, became friends once more, and united around the National Standard.

"And again I heard the mysterious voice say, 'Son of the Republic, look and learn.' At this, the dark, shadowy angel placed a trumpet to his mouth and blew three distinct blasts; and taking water from the ocean, he sprinkled it upon Europe, Asia, and Africa. Then my eyes beheld a fearful scene: From each of these countries arose thick, black clouds that were soon joined into one. And throughout this mass there gleamed a dark <u>red</u> light by which I saw hordes of armed men who moved with the cloud marching by land and sailing by sea to America, which country was enveloped in the volume of the cloud. And I dimly saw these vast armies devastate the whole country and burn the villages, towns and cities that I had beheld springing up. As my ears listened to the thundering of the cannon, clashing of swords and shouts and cries of millions in mortal combat, I again heard the mysterious voice saying, 'Son of the Republic, look and learn.' When the voice had ceased the dark shadowy angel placed his trumpet once more to his mouth and blew a long and fearful blast.

"Instantly light as of a thousand suns shone down from above me and pierced and broke into fragments the dark cloud which enveloped America. at the same moment the angel upon whose head still shone the word 'Union,' and who bore our national flag in one hand and a sword in the other, descended from heaven attended by legions of bright spirits. These immediately joined the inhabitants of America, who, I perceived, were well nigh overcome, but who, immediately taking courage again, closed up their broken ranks and renewed the battle. Again, amid the fearful noise of the conflict, I heard the mysterious voice saying, 'Son of the Republic, look and learn.' As the voice ceased, the shadowy angel for the last time dipped water from the ocean and sprinkled it upon America. Instantly the dark cloud rolled back, together with the armies it had brought, leaving the inhabitants of the land victorious.

"Then once more I beheld villages, towns and cities springing up where they had been before, while the bright angel, planting the azure standard he had brought into the midst of them cried with a loud voice: 'While the stars remain and the heavens send down dew upon the earth, so long shall the Republic last.' And taking from his brow the crown on which was blazoned the word 'Union,' he placed it upon the standard while the people, kneeling down, said 'Amen.'

"The scene instantly began to fade and dissolve and I at last saw nothing but the rising, curling vapor I at first beheld. This also disappearing, I found myself once more gazing upon my mysterious visitor, who, in the same voice I had heard before said, 'Son of the Republic, what you have seen is thus interpreted: Three great perils will come upon the Republic. The most fearful is the third, passing which the whole world united shall not prevail against her. <u>Let every child of the Republic learn to live for his God, his land and union.</u>' With these words the vision vanished, and I started from my seat and felt that I had seen a vision wherein had been shown me the birth, progress and destiny of the United States."

"Such, my friends," concluded the venerable narrator, "were the words I heard from Washington's own lips, and America will do well to profit by them."

Annex C

America's Future

From the Dream of General McClelland
(Somewhat Condensed)

This dream came to General McClelland at 2 o'clock of the third night after he came to Washington in command of the U.S. Army. The part applying to the present and future of the United States reads partly as follows:

"The dim, shadowy figure was no longer a dim, shadowy one, but the glorified refulgent figure of Washington, the Father of his Country and now for a second time its Savior. *** As I continued looking, an expression of sublime benignity came gently upon his visage and for the last time I heard that slow, solemn voice saying something like this: 'General McClelland while yet in the flesh I beheld the birth of the American Republic—It was indeed a hard and bloody one, but God's blessings were upon the nation, and therefore through this struggle for existence He sustained her with His mighty hand and brought her out triumphantly. A century has passed since then, and yet the child Republic has taken her position, a peer with nations whose pages of history extend for ages into the past. And now she has been brought to her second great struggle, this, so far the most perilous ordeal she has to endure. *** But her cries have come up out of the borders like sweet incense unto heaven. She will be saved. Then shall peace once more be upon her, and prosperity fill her with joy.

'BUT HER MISSION WILL NOT THEN BE FINISHED FOR ERE ANOTHER CENTURY SHALL HAVE GONE BY, the oppressors of the whole earth, hating and envying her and her exaltation, SHALL JOIN THEMSELVES TOGETHER AND RAISE UP THEIR HANDS AGAINST HER. But if she be found worthy of her high calling they shall surely be discomfited, and then will be ended her third and last struggle for existence.

'Let her in her prosperity, however, remember the Lord her God.

'Let her trust in Him and she shall never be confounded.'

59

The Warning

"…in the mouth of two or three witnesses every word may be established." Matthew 18:16

1   "With the monstrous weapons man already has, humanity is in danger of being trapped in this world by its moral adolescence. Our knowledge of science has clearly outstripped our capacity to control it.

We have too many men of science; too few men of God. We have grasped the mystery of the atom and rejected the Sermon on the Mount. Man is stumbling blindly through a spiritual darkness while toying with the precarious secrets of life and death.

The world has achieved brilliance without wisdom, power without conscience. Ours is a world of nuclear giants and ethical infants. We know more about war than we know about peace, more about killing than we know about living."

--Omar N. Bradley

* * * *

2   "…The old method of guerrilla warfare, as carried out from the hills and countryside, would be ineffective in a powerful country like the USA. Any such force would be wiped out within an hour. The new concept is to huddle as close to the enemy as possible so as to neutralize his modern and fierce weapons. This new concept creates conditions that involve the total community, whether they want to become involved or not. It sustains a state of confusion and the destruction of property. It dislocates the organs of harmony and order and reduces the central power to the level of a helpless sprawling octopus. During the hours of day, sporadic rioting takes place and massive sniping. Night brings all out warfare, organized fighting and unlimited terror against the oppressor and his forces.

"…the USA will become a bedlam of confusion and chaos be looted and destroyed… Essential pipelines will be severed and blown up and all manner of sabotage will occur. Violence and terror will spread like a firestorm. A clash will occur within the armed forces…Because of the vast area covered by the holocaust, U.S. forces will be spread too thin for effective action. Trucks and trains will not move the necessary supplies into the urban areas. The economy will fall into a state of chaos.

–Robert Williams, Leader, Revolutionary Action Movement (R.A.M.)

* * * *

3   When General William R. Dean was released from a Korean communist prison camp, the young Chinese psychologists who had been trying to break him said; "General, don't feel bad about leaving us. You know we will soon be with you. We are going to capture your country." Asked how, they replied; "We are going to destroy the moral character of a generation of your young Americans,

and when we have finished you will have nothing with which to really defend yourselves against us."

4   "To give (man) liberty but take from him his property which is the fruit and body of his liberty is to still leave him a slave.

--George Sutherland

* * * *

5   "Can the liberties of a nation be thought secure when we have removed their only firm basis, a conviction in the minds of the people that these liberties are of the gift of God? That they are not to be violated but with His wrath?"

--Thomas Jefferson

* * * *

6   "We have been the recipients of the choicest bounties of Heaven. We have been preserved, these many years, in peace and prosperity. We have grown in numbers, wealth, and power as no other nation has ever grown; but we have forgotten God. We have forgotten the gracious hand which preserved us in peace, and multiplied and enriched and strengthened us; and we have vainly imagined, in the deceitfulness of our hearts, that all these blessings were produced by some superior wisdom and virtue of our own. Intoxicated with unbroken success, we have become too self-sufficient to feel the necessity of redeeming and preserving grace, too proud to pray to the God that made us.

"It behooves us, then to humble ourselves before the offended Power, to confess our national sins, and to pray for clemency and forgiveness."

--Abraham Lincoln

* * * *

7   "Each of us has a natural right—from God—to defend his person, his liberty, and his property. These are the three basic requirements of life, and the preservation of any one of them is completely dependent upon the preservation of the other two. For what are our facilities but the extension of our individuality? And what is property but an extension of our faculties?"

--Frederick Bastiat "The Law"

* * * *

8   "Life, liberty, and property do not exist because men have made laws. On the contrary, it was the fact that life, liberty, and property existed beforehand that caused men to make laws in the first place."

-- Frederick Bastiat "The Law"

* * * *

9   "If men were angels, no government would be necessary. If angels were to govern men, neither external nor internal controls on government would be necessary."

-- James Madison

* * * *

10 "If the American people ever allow private banks to control the issue of currency, first by inflation, and then by deflation, the banks and corporations that will grow up around them, will deprive the people of all their property until their children will wake up homeless on the continent their fathers conquered."

-- Thomas Jefferson

* * * *

11 "We do not need more material development, we need more spiritual development. We do not need more intellectual power, we need more moral power. We do not need more knowledge, we need more character. We do not need more government, we need more culture. We do not need more law. We need more religion. We do not need more of the things that are seen, we need more of the things that are unseen. It is on that side of life that it is desirable to put the emphasis at the present time. If that side is strengthened, the other side will take care of itself. It is that side which is the foundation of all else. If the foundation be firm, the superstructure will stand."

--Calvin Coolidge

A Final Warning
The Mark

Since my first reading of the Book of Revelations, in my youth, I wondered how any one entity, The Beast or the Anti-Christ, could possibly gain control of every person on Earth and mark them as his own. That is no longer a mystery to me......The answer is debt.

Over the last few decades, many of the third world countries have fallen under the ownership of the "Beast".

It is done by the encouragement of the various countries to borrow vast amounts of monies from the World Bank and when the debt becomes too great for any one generation to pay the loan and accumulated interest, the debt is foreclosed on, for that country.

As there is no way to satisfy the debt, the owners of the World Bank require the indentured country to sign over all the Natural Resources under their domain.

ALL NATURAL RESOURCES, the only source of real wealth, land, timber, water, minerals, gold, silver, oil, gas, coal and all hunting and fresh or salt water fishing rights, anything of real wealth or value.

Money is not wealth. Only natural resources are wealth, when acted upon by the labor of men. For without natural resources a country is bankrupt. All commodities and trade necessary for survival come form natural resources, food, water, homes, vehicles, utilities, clothing, etc, etc.

Many of the smaller countries have already fallen into bondage and it would seem that America is about to follow with the other industrial nations.

Of course, the left wing socialists have already laid the groundwork for ownership of all natural resources in America by unconstitutional confiscation, that is timber, by the forest service, grazing land, by the BLM, park and national monuments, by the park service, all natural resources, by the department of natural resources (DNRC) this includes all water and all other lands, highways, ports and harbors, rivers, and inland waterways, etc, etc.

That has been done while the U.S. Constitution specifically limits government ownership to ten square miles for the seat of government, which is Washington D.C., see Section 8, Paragraph 17 of the U.S. Constitution.

All privately owned lands are also indentured with property taxes in most states. That is why the four sisters tried to remove property taxes for Montana residents. Property tax cannot be paid without income from natural resources.

Therefore, all natural resources, "owned" by the federal government in the various states or by lien thru property taxes, also subject to confiscation when our national debt is foreclosed on by the international bankers.

It must be understood that since 1913, the World Bank and its subsidiary bank here in America functioning under the guise of the "Federal" Reserve Bank are PRIVATELY OWNED by several of the wealthiest families on earth. They have corrupted the currency in most countries with <u>worthless</u> paper money issued at face value plus its compound interest which becomes the national debt.

Thomas Jefferson voiced the wisdom of the founders when he stated, "I believe that banking institutions are <u>more dangerous to our liberties</u> than standing armies. If the American people ever allow private banks to control the issue of their currency, first by inflation, then by deflation, the banks and corporations that will grow up around the banks will deprive the people of all property until their children wake-up homeless on the continent their fathers conquered."

The new bailout and stimulus packets have purposely brought our nation to the brink of bankruptcy and ready for foreclosure and ownership of all natural resources on planet earth by the international one-worlders. This is in preparation for "the mark" for no one can produce, buy, or sell anything without <u>permission</u> to use natural resources for our survival.

WHAT WILL YOU DO ABOUT IT?? IT IS PAST TIME TO DECIDE!!!

Remember, however, though the world must pass through a period of great tribulation, America will ultimately be set free as recorded in George Washington's vision, where myriads of bright spirits will descend from the heavens to assist us in our final battle. <u>AMERICA WILL ALWAYS REMAIN FREE.</u> That promise is more certain than tomorrow's sunrise!

The time is fast approaching when our Savior will appear;
    I wonder if He'll find us all prepared to greet him here?
Will all our lamps be found well filled, and shine with polish bright,
    Or will some wait till darkness comes—then grope around for light?

This is a glorious time to live, we must not fear or dread;
    'Tis true that trials 'wait us—but think what lies ahead!
I cannot picture grander things than all this Day does hold,
    In watching come to pass the words, God's prophets have foretold.

Have we the courage and the strength to hold our heads up high,
    And see above the faults of men, and keep a watchful eye?
Have we, the chosen ones of God, the faith to carry on
    Until the storms and troubles break to usher in the dawn?

His words divine—they do not change. God has a perfect plan;
    So watch, and be not led astray by false ideas of man.
Keep step with faith and join the ranks, which stand for truth and right—
    Then, when the sky grows dark, we'll know that just beyond is light.

--V.S. Lindsay

About the Author
Bill Koerner

Bill Koerner was born in Wisconsin and moved to St. Louis, Missouri when he was 6 years old where he attended school. Upon graduation, he worked as a commercial artist prior to entry into the service in 1949.

Bill served in the Army as Chief Warrant Officer and in the Military Intelligence Department. He saw action during the Vietnam War. In 1967 – 1968, he flew 253 combat missions as an aerial observer in Vietnam and saw extensive action during the TET Offensive.

Since his military retirement in 1969, he has been engaged in speaking on Constitutional principles before patriotic groups, state Legislatures, governors, and high schools and college students. He has worked on initiative petitions both in Utah and in Montana. He travels over the country appearing on radio and television as well as before live audiences. In Hamilton, Montana, he hosted his own television program, "The American Dream."

In the 1970's in Utah, Bill organized thousands of citizens into civil defense teams (Neighborhood Emergency Teams). The purpose of these teams was to enable the citizens to assume responsibility for their own safety in case of emergencies or insurrectionist activities.

Since Bill has made his home in Montana, he has been active in local civic organizations and has served 8 years as city judge.

For further information, write to:

The American Dream
P.O. Box 387
Corvallis, Montana 59828

Individual Rights & Delegated Authority

The primary responsibility of government is to protect the individual, God given rights to life, liberty, and property for when government protects individual rights it automatically protects society because society is made up of individuals.

However, when individual rights are sacrificed to satisfy majority or mob rule, all society suffers the loss of all rights and freedoms.

Government derives its power to govern through delegated authority form the individual citizens it governs. The individual citizen cannot do an illegal activity, such as robbing their neighbor for personal needs without breaking the law; they therefore cannot delegate authority to government to break the law for them.

When government steals in that manner it is called legalized plunder for that is still robbery and no amount of majority support, fifty-one percent or even ninety-nine percent, can make it lawful.